The World's Best Known Marketing Secret

Building Your Business by Referral

4th Edition

Ivan Misner, Ph.D.

Mike Macedonio

Paradigm Publishing
in conjunction with
Beneath the Cover Press

The World's Best-Known Marketing Secret
Building Your Business By Referral

Copyright © 1994, 1999, 2000, 2011 by Ivan R. Misner, Ph.D.

Printed in the United States of America

Beneath the Cover Press
A Paradigm Productions Book

To order the book, contact your local bookstore or call 800-688-9394

Publisher's Cataloging-In-Publication Data
(Prepared by The Donohue Group, Inc.)

Misner, Ivan R., 1956-
  The world's best-known marketing secret : building your business by referral / Ivan Misner [and] Mike Macedonio. — 4th ed.
    p. ; cm.
  Originally published: Austin, TX : Bard Press, c1994.
  "A Paradigm Productions book."—T.p. verso.
  Includes index.
  ISBN: 978-0-9740819-3-9
  1. Marketing. 2. Word-of-mouth advertising. I. Macedonio, Mike. II. Title.
HF5415 .M573 2011
658.8   2011909478

The author may be contacted at the following address:

  BNI—Business Network Int'l.
  545 College Commerce Way
  Upland, CA 91786
  909-608-7575

Copyediting: *Jeff Morris, Julien Sharp*   Jacket Design: *Media Makers*
Proofreading: *Deborah Costenbader*   Index: *Linda Webster*
Text Design/Production: *Hespenheide Design*

First Edition   **Revised Edition**
First printing: August 1994   First printing: March 2000
Second printing: September 1994   Second printing: June 2001
Third printing: December 1995   Third printing: July 2002
Fourth printing: August 1997   Fourth printing: July 2003
                                                    Fifth printing: January 2005

Second Edition   **Fourth Edition**
First printing: March 1999   April 2011

Table of Contents

Endorsements

"This is one book you cannot afford to overlook! From beginning to end, *The World's Best Known Marketing Secret* is a MUST READ. It outlines the only marketing strategy in existence that is both highly economical and powerfully effective, no matter what business you're in or where you live."

—Susan RoAne, author of *How To Work a Room®* and *The Secrets of Savvy Networking*

1

The Best Way to Grow Your Business

The Advantages of Referrals

Marketing Reality Check

It's reality-check time. How many ways are there for you to increase your business? Dozens? Hundreds? Maybe thousands? Guess again. Try four. That's right — there are only four main strategies that you can incorporate to increase your business. What — you don't believe us? Then read on.

First, you can advertise. Oh yes, we know: there are many different ways you can advertise. There's radio, newspaper, magazine, and direct mail advertising. You can advertise on billboards, TV, park benches, pens, balloons, or leaflets. If you feel really daring, you can even try skywriting. But when the dust settles and the smoke clears, it's still advertising.

Every business we've ever known, including those we have personally worked in or owned, has advertised in one form or another. Traditional forms of advertising, however, can be expensive. For example, the average one-time cost for a four-inch by four-inch advertising display in a major metropolitan newspaper is several thousand dollars.

If you were to run a $2,200 advertisement only once a week for one full year, you'd spend over $100,000. Assuming that the newspaper gave you a volume discount of 25 percent, you would still spend tens of thousands. For virtually all start-up companies, as well as many companies that have been in business for a few years and untold numbers of other long-established businesses, this kind of expense is not feasible.

We are not suggesting that you stop advertising. Depending on your product or service, many forms of it can be very effective for you. But it doesn't matter whether you're Procter & Gamble or the corner florist — you don't have an unlimited budget to spend on advertising. Therefore, you choose your advertising options according to a somewhat fixed budget, and off you go. The real question is, "Does your advertising bring in all the business you need or would like?"

Ask yourself, "Am I making more money than I want because of the tremendous amount of business that advertising has generated for me or my company?" If the answer is no, then you need to increase your advertising budget. If you can't increase your advertising budget, then you need to adopt another strategy.

Competition for customers in our society is fierce. Your competitors are trying to win over the same clients or customers that you are. Even in a strong economy, advertising does not guarantee success over your competitors. The people you're trying to reach, by some estimates, are bombarded by thousands of advertising messages per day. This constant inundation means that your prospects potentially have many alternative sources of supply for the products or services you provide.

In a tough economy, advertising may not work at all. When times are especially tough, you and your competitors are effectively competing for a reduced pool of available dollars, and people are more value-conscious about the dollars they *do* spend.

The second way to increase your business is through a public relations (PR) campaign. This can be very effective, but it can also be very expensive and time-consuming for a small company. Large companies hire PR firms, but this doesn't really help develop the credibility of the individual sales rep out in the field. Therefore, if your company is too small to hire a PR firm, or if you are a sales rep for a large firm, you need to create your own personalized PR program.

A good PR program can enhance your credibility, which in turn will have a positive impact on your referral marketing opportunities. In Chapter 10, we will discuss the importance of a good PR program to support your referral marketing efforts. However, it is important to understand that PR only lays the groundwork for a sale; it rarely *closes* the sale. While its importance should not be underestimated, you should know that it rarely makes a quick difference in your bottom line. Therefore, no business can rely primarily on its public relations effort.

The third way to increase your business is through referral. Referral marketing has long been recognized as the most cost-effective form of marketing a business can use. Tom Peters, author of *Thriving on Chaos*, regards referral marketing as one of the major ways a business can bring in new clients or customers. Peters asserts that one has to be, "just as organized, thoughtful, and systematic about *[referral marketing]*" as with other forms of advertising and marketing, yet, "You never see a *[referral]* section in marketing plans." Peters says that if you don't have a well-structured plan, you are not likely to have impressive results.

Four Ways to Market Your Business

Marketing Strategy	Initial Goal	Ultimate Goal	Cost	Advantages
Advertising/ Online	Create awareness and leads	Image in marketplace and sales	Could be big dollars for media	Target or wide coverage
Public Relations	Create awareness	Image in marketplace and some sales	Big dollars for public relations specialists	Wide coverage
Referrals	Generate	Sales	Staff time	Target or wide coverage; efficient, extended impact; inexpensive; quality customers
Cold Calling	Generate sales through direct contact	Sales	Substantial staff time, shoe leather, and patience	(We tried ... but we just can't name any advantages here!)

Unfortunately, as we said earlier, most marketing surveys have shown that consumers are ten times more likely to talk about you if they are unhappy or unsatisfied with your service than if they are happy or satisfied. The best way to get truly impressive results is to have a plan and develop a structured program.

(We do have to mention one other marketing strategy that a lot of people use as an alternative to advertising and PR, and that is . . . cold calling! Yes, that's right — the "C word!" Just mentioning it makes us shiver. Given the other options, who in his right mind would want to spend the rest of his professional life *cold calling*?)

So . . . this is your marketing reality check.

Of these four strategies for increasing and enhancing your business, we'd have to recommend advertising as the most immediately effective means of getting the message out about your business. However, most businesses have a limited budget to spend on advertising. PR is really best used only in conjunction with other marketing efforts, and we don't know about you, but many years ago we promised ourselves we would never do a cold call ever again for as long as we live!

That leaves only one other way that you can effectively build your business: by referral!

A Cost-Effective Form of Advertising

Referral marketing is a form of advertising and, like media advertising, requires careful planning to achieve a worthwhile return for your time and energy. As you begin to use and benefit by referral marketing, you will see that it is a very cost-effective medium. If you haven't developed a structured referral-marketing program to generate business, then you can't enjoy its benefits.

While many business executives and entrepreneurs recognize the value of referrals to their respective organizations, they are not clear on how to consistently generate a large number of referrals. Worse, they don't realize that there is a segment of the population looking for their product or service *right now*.

People Want Referrals

People from all walks of life want referrals — not just the business community, but the general public, as well. Few people want to choose a dentist, for example, from a printed advertisement. People want to have more personal information before making such selections.

People don't want to go to the telephone book to pick a lawyer. People don't want to pick a real estate agent from the Yellow Pages. Nor do they want to find an accountant, a chiropractor, an insurance agent, a dentist, or a mechanic that way. People want referrals from trusted sources!

Historically, the only problem has been linking the people who need services or products with the people who provide them. A structured referral marketing campaign begins by acknowledging that there is a segment of the public that wants you and *your* service as badly as you want *their* business.

The general public has no idea what they are going to get when they hire someone through an ad. For instance, years ago, a San Diego bank hired a private investigator to track down a bank robber and retrieve stolen funds. The search led to Mexico. The investigator crossed the border and then, realizing he would need a Spanish interpreter, opened up the telephone book and hired the first interpreter listed in the Yellow Pages.

After many days, the investigator finally captured the bandit and, through the interpreter, asked him, "Where did you hide the money?" In Spanish, the thief replied, "What money? I have no idea what you're talking about."

With that, the investigator drew his pistol, pointed it at the suspect, and said to the interpreter, "Tell him that if he doesn't tell me where the money is, I will shoot him where he stands."

Upon receiving this message, the bank robber said to the interpreter, "Señor, I have hidden the money in a coffee can, under the fourth floorboard, in the second-floor men's room of the Palacio Hotel on Via Del Rio in La Paz."

"What did he say?" the investigator asked the interpreter.

"Señor," said the interpreter, after he thought for a moment, "he says he is prepared to die like a man!"

Whenever you choose a professional exclusively from an advertisement and have no other source of information, you may be taking a big risk as to the quality of service you will receive. When you work with a person referred to you by someone you know and trust, the risk is greatly reduced. Someone else has done business with that person and is recommending that professional to you with confidence.

Referrals Are Good Business

Compare a lead that you receive from an advertisement with a similar lead (that is, referral) that you get from someone you know. The referred lead is easier to close and costs less to obtain. Often, the referral provides a higher-quality client or customer with less chance of misunderstanding or disappointment. When we asked business owners why referral business is better than the business they get from ads they have placed, they say the referred business —

- is easier to close
- will generate on average five times more revenue in the first year
- has the lowest acquisition cost
- is more likely to refer other clients
- has far fewer objections
- has a stronger sense of loyalty
- remains a client longer
— and most important of all —
- has a higher sense of trust

This last point is particularly important. Relying on the advice of a mutual friend or acquaintance, the referral starts with a higher level of trust for you and your product or service. Getting dozens of people to send such referrals your way every day is what building a successful referral-based business is all about — and this book will show you how to do just that!

Advertisements That Tout Their Referrals

Why is it that while most businesses have some sort of plan for their advertising program, few have a plan for generating business via referral marketing?

Ironically, some companies focus on how effective referral marketing has been for them — right in their advertisements. It's as if they were saying to prospective customers, "Most of the time, we don't need to pay for advertisements like this one because we get so many customers from referrals. Lucky for you, we decided to run this ad, in case you don't know any of our current customers."

A radio ad we once heard was sponsored by a medium-sized commercial bank. In the ad, the bank asked the question, "Would you refer your bank to a friend?" They bragged that they got most of their new customers from referrals from their existing customers. This company recognized the value of their referral business, so much so that they felt compelled to incorporate it into their advertising campaign.

Recently, we heard another radio ad for a local business. They spent 50 of 60 seconds discussing how important referral marketing was to their operations. During the last ten seconds, they announced that over 80 percent of all their business came through referrals, with the remaining 20 percent of their customers coming from "advertisements like this one!" Sometimes you wonder if such advertisers really do have strong referrals, or are just trying to cash in on the aura of having it.

In this chapter we reviewed the four ways to market your business and the importance of a referral-based business. In the next chapter, we are going to show you how you can actually create your own referral marketing plan in order to make the most effective use of this valuable concept.

⇒ *Action Items*

1. List everything you currently do to increase your business (advertising, PR, cold calling, referrals).
2. Track the monetary cost and time cost for each method.
3. Track the business acquired from each method.

2

Referrals and Referral Marketing, Networking, Word of Mouth, Buzz, Viral Marketing . . .

What Does It All Mean?

The many terms associated with marketing can get a little blurry with so many different interpretations.

Before moving further, we would like to discuss how some of these terms are used and what our interpretations are. After clarifying these sometimes overused terms, we can then begin working with you to create a plan to build your business by referral. Our intention is not to claim to have the right definitions or declare ownership of the terms. We would simply like to start by looking at some of the widely used definitions and clarify how we will be using the terms.

> Networking is the process of developing and using contacts to increase your business, enhance your knowledge, expand your sphere of influence, or serve the community.

One term that seems to have multiple meanings is **networking**. For some, this is about going out and collecting a huge database of names, usually by collecting business cards. Others see networking as the opportunity to get in front of people and be able to personally prospect them for business. There are others that perceive networking as nothing more than schmoozing and boozing, with no specific intention except to be seen and socialize. To us, networking is the process of developing and using contacts to increase your business, enhance your knowledge, expand your sphere of influence, or serve the community.

To be successful with business networking, you should understand that it is really about helping others as a way of growing your business. The people you help are more willing to help you or connect you to people they know. In essence, networking is part of the process you go through to build your referral-based business. Through networking you can deliver your positive message effectively. Referrals are the end result.

It's important to define **referral** at this point. A referral is a recommendation of a person or business to someone who has a need for your products or services and is willing to connect.

Referral marketing is one of the most powerful techniques you can use to succeed in almost any venture. People network both formally and informally as a way of accomplishing these objectives.

As we discuss networking throughout this book, keep in mind that it is networking for the express purpose of building a referral-based business.

One term that is often interchanged with referral marketing is **word of mouth**. In fact, we have used this term quite often over the course of our professional careers. However, as the concept of referral marketing developed over the years, we have come to believe that word of mouth is just a component of referral marketing, rather than synonymous with it. For this reason, in this book and everywhere else we discuss our marketing focus, we will define word of mouth as simply what people are saying about your products or services. A word-of-mouth marketing plan would have an effective message, delivered through identified Referral Sources to a targeted audience. Word of mouth ties in very closely with customer service, as we will discuss in the next chapter.

We should also take a quick look at **network marketing**. This term is often used in multi-level marketing organizations to describe their selling system. This type of marketing would have distributors sign up other distributors to sell their products or services and who would also sign up other distributors. In this system, the "up-line" of distributors receives commissions on the distributors below them.

Marketing buzz, or just **buzz,** is a term used in referral marketing. The interaction of

> A **referral** is the recommendation of a person or business to someone who has a need for your products or services and is willing to connect.

> **Word of mouth** is simply what people are saying about your products or services. A word-of-mouth marketing plan would have an effective message, delivered through identified Referral Sources to a targeted audience.

> **Network marketing** This term is often used in multi-level marketing organizations to describe their marketing system. This type of marketing would have distributors sign up other distributors to sell their products or services and who would also sign up other distributors. In this system, the up-line of distributors would receive commissions on the distributors below them.

Marketing buzz (or just buzz) This is a term used in word-of-mouth marketing. The interaction of consumers and users of a product or service serve to amplify the original marketing message.

Referral Marketing is a business strategy to attract new customers or clients through a process of building relationships, which results in a flow of personally recommended business.

consumers and users of a product or service serve to amplify the original marketing message.

Viral marketing and **viral advertising** refer to marketing techniques that use pre-existing social networks to create increases in brand awareness or to achieve other marketing objectives (such as product sales) through self-replicating viral processes. This is the trend where everyone is talking about the latest fashion, movie, or hot spot.

In this book we are going to show you how to create and implement a comprehensive Referral Marketing Plan to build your business, so the term *referral marketing,* as we will approach it, is a business strategy to attract new customers or clients through a process of building relationships, which results in a flow of personally-recommended business.

We will be using networking as a tool in your Referral Marketing Plan.

3

Business By Referral

The Concept and the Attitude that Make the Difference

The Paradox

What if there were a way to build your business, year in and year out, regardless of fluctuations in the economy or the activities of your competition? There *is* a way: it's called *referral marketing*.

Referral marketing is a paradox. It is a component of what we call "the world's best known marketing secret." How, you may be wondering, can anything be the "best known" and a "secret" at the same time? Therein lies the paradox: virtually everyone recognizes the phrase and its importance to the average businessperson, yet those same individuals are often far less clear on the specifics of harnessing this all-too-elusive commodity.

Referral marketing is one of the world's most effective, yet least understood, marketing strategies. Although the concept of marketing a business by referral is universally recognized among marketing experts, it is seldom covered in popular or instructional books on business marketing. Such books will maybe make a fleeting reference to the concept, but almost never provide details on how you can actually develop good referrals for your business. The few authors who do mention it either fail to provide a clear, concise, well-structured plan for the typical executive or entrepreneur to follow, or they focus on a much too narrow aspect of the process.

The W-O-M Factor

Many business professionals make the mistake of thinking that developing business by referral is simply about providing "good customer service."

Good customer service is a prerequisite for long-term business success, but good customer service alone will not develop the volume of business that can be generated by referral marketing. The reason for this is something that we call the Word-of-Mouth Factor (or W-O-M Factor). The W-O-M Factor has three related parts:

1. People are more likely to talk about your company when they are unhappy than when they are happy or satisfied.
2. Therefore, good customer service generally does more to reduce negative word of mouth than it does to substantially increase referrals.
3. Thus, to increase your business through referrals, you must do more than increase the quality of your customer service: you must increase your positive word-of-mouth marketing.

In essence, good customer service can reduce *negative* word of mouth, but to significantly increase your business volume, you need to do more than increase the quality of your customer service: you need to be skilled at referral marketing.

Good customer service is a prerequisite for long-term business success, but good customer service alone will not develop the volume of business that can be generated by referral marketing.

A study conducted by a West Coast market research firm found that dissatisfied automobile customers tell 22 others about their experience. A Texas-based research firm discovered that dissatisfied bank customers tell 11 other people, and each will, in turn, tell five others. In other words, one unhappy customer results in 66 others hearing about the dissatisfaction, and you can bet that the 55 people in the 'second generation' hear a whopper.

If this is even partially true, and we see no reason to believe otherwise, then good customer service, at best, helps reduce or eliminate negative word of mouth, while perhaps making a small contribution to positive word of mouth. Yet too many entrepreneurs, especially first-time entrepreneurs, mistakenly believe that simply providing an excellent product or service ought to be enough to induce people to flock to their door.

Business By Referral: The Fundamental Strategies

As we have been discussing in this chapter, according to popular business lore, somehow positive word of mouth about a business will circulate sufficiently among the right targets on its own. This is wishful thinking. The effect doesn't occur fast enough to enable a business to grow at a brisk pace. The inescapable conclusion to all this is that if you want to have a solid referral-based business, you have to take steps to generate it yourself.

Below are the two key strategies that are the major components of this book. In order for any businessperson to create a prosperous referral business, he or she must accomplish two things:

1. Develop a powerful, diverse network of contacts.
2. Create a positive message, delivered effectively.

To be successful in business today, you need an edge. This means that you need to be very creative in order to be competitive. Creativity in marketing your business has become a basic tenet for today's successful company or professional practice.

Here's a great example: three storeowners shared adjacent storefronts in the same building. Times were tough. In hopes of picking up sales, the storeowner at one end of the building put a sign over his front entrance that announced, "YEAR-END CLEARANCE!!!" At the other end of the building, a second owner responded with his own sign: "ANNUAL CLOSE-OUT!"

The storeowner in the middle knew that he had to act fast or he'd lose a lot of business. After careful consideration, he hung a larger sign over his front door that read, "MAIN ENTRANCE."

The moral of this story: you can't control the economy. You can't control your competition. But you can control *your response* to the economy. And you can control *your response* to your competition.

Your Response to the Economy and to Your Competition

The first step in building a referral-based business is to understand that you control your response to the things around you. I have traveled around the country giving presentations to thousands of business people on how to develop business by referral. On one trip I attended an after-hours business mixer in Hartford, Connecticut. At the time, this area was in a severe recession, and the only topic of discussion seemed to be how bad business was. The whole affair was depressing because nearly everyone was obsessed with the problems of the economy and its impact on their business.

I was introduced to one of the many real estate agents attending. Given the decrease in property values in the region, I was leery of asking this gentleman the standard, "How's business?" question. I didn't want to hear yet another variation of how the world was coming to an end. He shared with me, though, that he was having a great year. Naturally, I was surprised, and asked, "You did say you were in real estate, didn't you?"

"Yes."

"We are in Connecticut, aren't we?"

"Yes," he said with a slight grin.

"And you're having a good year?" I asked.

"I'm actually having my best year ever!"

"Your best year!" I said in amazement. After thinking for a moment I asked him, "Is this your first year in real estate?"

"No," he replied with a laugh, "I've been in real estate for almost ten years."

I asked him why he was doing so well, given the conditions of the economy and the stiff competition. He reached into his pocket and pulled out a blue-and-white badge:

> I ABSOLUTELY REFUSE
> TO PARTICIPATE
> IN THE RECESSION!!!

"That's your secret?" I asked. "You refuse to participate in the recession, so business is booming?"

"That's correct. While most of my competitors are crying the blues about how bad business is, I'm out drumming up tons of business through referrals."

Considering what he said, I looked around the room and eavesdropped for a moment on people complaining about how slow business was. While nearly all were commiserating with one another, I concluded that very few were actually seeking new business. As a result, very little business was being accomplished. If you want to do well in business, you must understand that it does absolutely no good to complain to people about tough times. When you complain about how terrible business has been for you, half the people don't care and the other half are glad that you're worse off than they are!

— DR. IVAN MISNER

A self-fulfilling prophecy on a mass scale can be hard to change. Attitudes are contagious, both positive and negative. Be positive, and surround yourself with positive professionals.

We are convinced that if you want to stand out from your competition, the worst thing to do is to cry the blues along with them. While you cannot control the economy or your competition, like the Ivan's Hartford realtor and the owner of the store in the middle with the huge sign, you can most definitely control your response to the economy and to your competition. If you let outside forces paralyze your actions, you will fail. Your attitude affects your income!

As we'll explore throughout this book, one of the single most effective ways that you can take charge of your situation independent of the fluctuations of the economy is to gain an edge over your competition by mastering the skills of referral marketing.

⇒ *Action Items*

1. Give up the notion that good customer service alone will increase your business.
2. Write out your new response to the economy, competition, interest rates, government bureaucracy, or any other place you have been directing your blame.

4

Finding Your
Starting Point

If you have little or no experience with referral marketing, it would be a mistake to jump into action without preparing yourself. Central to the referral marketing process is getting people to actually *give* you referrals. To do so, they must know exactly what you do — what product or service you provide or make, how and under what conditions you provide it, how well you do it, and in what ways you are better at what you do than your competitors. You have to communicate this information to your sources. And to communicate effectively, you must know the same things.

> If you can't tell your potential sources what you do or what you sell, how can they give you good referrals?

It may seem like a no-brainer; don't we all know what we do for a living? Yes, of course, most of us do. But can you communicate it clearly and simply to your potential sources? When you try to do so, you may find that you're not quite as clear on the facts as you thought — and if you can't tell your potential sources what you do or what you sell, how can they send you good referrals?

Before you map out where you're going to take your business with your referral marketing plan, pause and get a clear picture of where your business stands today. Try to answer, in simple terms, the following questions:

- Why are you in business?
- What do you sell?
- Who are your customers?
- How well do you compete?

Answering these questions for yourself will help you tell others what your business is about. This will make you more effective at implementing your own comprehensive and systematic referral system.

Know Your Mission

You may think you know why you're in business, but perhaps it's been years since you gave it serious thought. Now is a good time to reexamine why you're doing what you're doing. Ask yourself the following questions:

- What is my business mission?
  Beyond simply making a living, what are my long-range professional goals? Do I wish to become the standard by which my competitors are judged? Is it my dream to help make the world a better place?
- Where is my organization going?
  Am I achieving my mission? Am I making plans to accomplish it? How can I change policies, procedures, or human resources to improve my chances of achieving my mission?
- What environment is my organization operating in?
  What are the social, economic, and technological trends that affect the way I do business and my progress toward my goals?
- What are my core competencies?
  What do I like to do? What is it that I do better than my competitors? Is my business mission compatible with my values and aptitudes?

As business consultants, we've seen too many business professionals and companies try to be all things to all people. They usually start out with the fundamentally sound goal of finding a niche that will make them successful, but they often go astray by changing direction every time a customer, advisor, or associate suggests a new product or service. The mission gets lost in a frantic scramble for business before the original idea ever gets a chance to pay off. We advise such companies to pause periodically to analyze their business and, if necessary, refocus on their mission and philosophy.

Ivan took his own advice when he founded BNI (Business Network International) in 1985. He determined that BNI's primary mission would be to pass business referrals to its members, specifically, "To help our members increase their business through a structured, positive, and professional word-of-mouth program."*

---

*Now becoming known as a referral marketing program

Since 1985, many people have brought BNI worthy ideas for new activities, programs, and projects that might help members in other ways. Although these are often very good ideas, many simply are not within BNI's focus. There are better companies, educational programs, and institutions than BNI, for example, to provide specialized sales and marketing training.

Some years ago, several BNI Directors brought an idea to Ivan: to have BNI create a referral-training program that could substantially help business people improve their referral success. Although on the surface this looked like a great compliment to what BNI did, in the end it did not pass Ivan's BNI mission test. There was value to the idea and a need in the marketplace, but it simply wasn't part of BNI's mission and did not become part of BNI's business. What Ivan did do with the idea was to partner with me, helping my team and me to build a referral training company that is now known as the Referral Institute. The two organizations, BNI and Referral Institute, have a powerful strategic alliance, while BNI has stayed true to its mission.

— **MIKE MACEDONIO**

BNI has rigorously avoided implementing new ideas, even very worthwhile projects, that are not directly related to its mission or that would change its focus. We believe that this is one of the reasons why BNI has become the world's largest and most successful referral marketing organization in such a relatively short time.

Know Your Products and Services

When your Referral Marketing Plan is working well, prospective customers buy from you the first time because they have been referred by your sources. They may continue to buy from you because they trust you and have developed a good relationship with you. But whatever the reasons for which they come, and whatever the reasons for which they stay, they are your customers primarily because they need your products or services.

A clear idea of your range of products or services is something your sources need to communicate to prospects. For each product or service you plan to market during your referral marketing campaign, you must be able to articulate for your sources the answers to the following questions:

- What is the purpose of your product or service? What needs does it satisfy?
- How would you describe it? What are its shape, size, functions, key features, principal activities, benefits?
- How is your product or service delivered to the customer?
- How much does it cost, and under what conditions (geographic location, complexity of the work, tools required, etc.)?

There are other questions concerning your products or services that you should answer for your own strategic purposes. Is your product becoming obsolete? Is there a newer or better way to provide the same service? What are the social and environmental effects of your product or service? Will economic or regulatory trends force you to change your products or services or the conditions under which you provide them? In the long term, will you be satisfied to continue to offer these products or services?

Know Your Target Market

What is your target market? Most simply defined, it is the specific set of customers whose needs you are trying to meet. This is the audience, out of all those who might hear your message, for whom you design your marketing program. Instead of trying to sell your product or service to everyone in a market — everyone in your town, for example, or everyone who might see your television commercial — you should aim your message toward those who have the greatest potential need or desire for your product or service.

Even though you're pretty sure who your customers are, it's always good practice to step back now and then and examine your assumptions. You should be able to answer these questions for your sources:

- Who are your most likely customers?
- What do your customers come to you for?
- What is your real specialty, your area of expertise?
- What segment of your business gives you the most pleasure and the most profit?

Answering these questions will also give you a head start when you plan your referral strategy. Where should you concentrate your referral-gathering efforts? If you're a travel agent specializing in Caribbean cruises, your target audience is more likely to be found on the rosters of the American Association of Retired Persons than on those of Greenpeace. Should you publicize your services on talk shows? Trade shows? Street fairs? It depends on the themes of those gatherings. Examine every event, every opportunity, to see whether your target audience is likely to be well-represented. Then concentrate your marketing efforts where they will be most effective.

We would like to let you know about a wonderful online resource called Networking Now. NetworkingNow.com has over 200 downloadable PDF Articles, Business Articles, Training Modules, MP3 Audio Files, Videos, AND Digital Books as part of its downloadable library!

Subscribers to this online service receive full access to all online and downloadable content. The site's highly specialized downloadable documents and audio files contain a wealth of networking knowledge from many of the world's masters of networking. From the day you subscribe, you will receive full access to all content that is restricted to subscribers of the site.

To get you started, we would like to present you a special offer: a 6-month free subscription to NetworkingNow.com! To activate your free subscription, go to www.networkingnow.com and hit the "Subscribe Now" button. Select the 6-Month Premium Subscription. Enter coupon code "referralinstitute" and hit "Update Cart." This will create a 0 balance. Click on "Check Out Now." Enter contact information and create a password. You will be asked to enter credit card information. No charges will be made if you cancel your subscription within six months. Click on "Place Order" to complete the subscription.

On future visits you can enter through the member login by putting in your email address and password. Once logged in, hit the "Audio" button and select the audio titled *Finding Your Starting Point Networking Café Telebridge*.

Know Your Competitive Position

To find out how you stack up against your competition, take a little time to analyze your competitive status. This exercise will help your understand

and emphasize your unique selling position. How do you differ, and how can you position yourself for best competitive advantage?

In his book *Networking Like A Pro,* Ivan explained this method of finding your competitive position: "Your Unique Selling Proposition (USP) is basically a brief description of the purpose of your business, stated in the most succinct and compelling way possible in order to get others to understand the unique value of what you do. A good USP simply tells people what you do, in a manner that gets them to ask how you do it."

There's no single formula for conducting a competitive analysis; it's mostly just good business sense. Try to stay aware of what your competition is doing and how your business stacks up against it. For example:

- Are your prices and costs competitive — do customers who compare costs come back to you?
- Do you compete effectively in terms of product or service quality?
- Are you seen as the vendor of choice — why do people seek you out?
- Are you growing, losing ground, or just holding onto your market share?
- Are you waiting to see what will happen and hoping to react in time?

Staying competitive also implies being aware of trends and reacting to changes faster than your competitors. How will changes in technology and society affect the competition? Are your products or services more advanced than those of your competition? Do your competitors have the jump on you with online marketing? Understanding the driving forces in your industry — growth rates, shifts in buyer demographics, product and marketing innovations, the entry or exit of other competitors, changes in cost or efficiency, and so forth — will make you a top competitor.

Five Keys to a Competitive Strategy

Your competitive strategy consists of the approaches and initiatives you take to attract customers, withstand competitive pressures, and strengthen your market position. As discussed by Arthur Thompson and A. J. Strickland in *Strategic Management: Concepts and Cases,* there are five competitive strategies you should consider:

1. **A low-cost leader strategy:** Strive to be the overall low-cost provider of a product or service that appeals to a broad range of customers. Notable examples are Sam's Club for general merchandise; Best Buy for electronics, appliances, and media items; and Southwest Airlines for air travel.
2. **A broad differentiation strategy:** Seek to differentiate the company's product offerings from those of its rivals in ways that will appeal to a broad range of buyers. Nordstrom is known for its customer service policies and personnel; Whole Foods has established itself as a major food retailer with an emphasis on health foods and organic groceries.
3. **A best-cost provider strategy:** Give customers more value for the money by emphasizing both low cost and upscale difference, with a goal to keep costs and prices lower than those of other providers of comparable quality and features. The Saturn division of General Motors has managed to produce an economy car with customer satisfaction ratings that rival those of much more expensive cars.
4. **A focused or market-niche strategy based on lower cost:** Concentrate on a narrow buyer segment and outcompeting rivals on the basis of lower cost. The Gap is an example of this strategy.
5. **A focused or market-niche strategy based on differentiation:** Offer niche members a product or service customized to their tastes and requirements. Rolls Royce sells a limited number of custom-built cars at the high end of the automobile prestige spectrum; big and tall shops specialize in selling mainstream styles to a limited market with specific physical requirements.

The Next Step

By now, you should have a pretty clear idea of how to tell others your business mission, the nature of your products and services, the people who constitute your target market, and the way you stack up against the competition. The ability to communicate this information to your sources and prospects will be invaluable as you begin to build your network and formulate your plan to gain more and more business the most effective way — through referrals.

⇛ *Action Items*

After reading this chapter, you should be able to answer the following questions:

1. What is my business mission?
2. Beyond simply making a living, what are my long-range professional goals?
3. Where is my organization going?
4. Am I achieving my mission, or am I making plans to accomplish it?
5. How can I change policies, procedures, or personnel to improve my chances of achieving my mission?
6. What environment is my organization operating in — what are the social, economic, and technological trends that affect the way I do business and my progress toward my goals?
7. What are my core competencies — what do I like to do?
8. What is it that I do better than my competitors?
9. Is my business mission compatible with my values and aptitudes?
10. What is the purpose of my product or service — what needs does it satisfy?
11. How would I describe my product or service — what are its shape, size, functions, key features, principal activities, and benefits?
12. How is my product or service delivered to the customer?
13. How much does my product or service cost, and under what conditions?
14. Who are my most likely customers and what do they come to me for?
15. What segment of my business gives me the most pleasure and the most profit?
16. Are my prices and costs competitive — do customers who compare costs come back to me, and do I compete effectively in terms of product or service quality?
17. Am I seen as the vendor of choice — why do people seek me out?
18. Am I growing, losing ground, or just holding onto my market share?

5

Networking vs. Direct Prospecting

If you're getting all the referrals you need, does this mean you don't need to sell anymore? Only if you don't want to eat!

Anybody who's experienced and successful in referral marketing will tell you that sales skills are absolutely required. They're needed in every part of the process — not just in closing the sale with the prospect.

First, you have to sell yourself to your potential Referral Source — she has to buy the concept that there's value in introducing you to someone she knows. It's important to remember also that a referral is not a guaranteed sale. It's the opportunity to do business with someone you have been recommended to — you still have to close the deal — most of the time. You have to make it clear that you know how to sell, that you can and will provide the products or services you are expected to provide, and that your customer will be happy with both the process and the result. Your ability to deliver these things will all reflect favorably on the provider of the referral. If you can't make that first "sale," your potential referral provider probably won't give you any referrals, because he or she won't be inclined to risk his or her relationship with the prospect. That is, he or she won't do his or her part to sell the referral.

Two separate doctoral studies, one from California in the early '90s and one from Florida in 2006, found that approximately 34 percent of all business referrals turn into sales. This is an outstanding number, but it's still not 100 percent. Therefore, sales skills are still important in networking. Some people are better at closing sales than others. Having the knowledge and skill to generate the referral, and then having the knowledge and skill to close the sale, gives the businessperson a one-two punch.

Second, you have to sell yourself to the prospect in order to get that first appointment. Yes, the referral helps a great deal, but you've still got to convince the prospect that the appointment is worth his or her time and likely to result in a favorable outcome. You should avoid being aggressive, indecisive, or evasive at this point. Having been in contact with your referral provider, the prospect is expecting a high level of respect and professionalism in your approach. You can and should be confident that a mutually beneficial deal is in the works, and you should communicate this to the prospect by your attitude and actions. Strive not to embarrass your Referral Source. Third, once you have made the appointment, you of course have to make the target sale: you have to persuade the prospect to buy your product or service. (This is what usually comes to mind when one hears the word "sale." As you can see, it's not the only aspect, even though it may be the most important to your bottom line in the short term.) *Your integrity is paramount at this stage.* The prospect should know exactly what to expect — no hidden charges, no unexpected exceptions, and no bait-and-switch.

If you've created a highly efficient system of generating referrals for your business, you will see a steady stream of referrals being funneled to you. This does not guarantee that you will be capable of closing any of them. You'll need sales skills to turn prospects into new clients, customers, or patients.

Note, however, that in referral marketing, closing the deal with your prospect is neither the beginning nor the end of the selling process. In order to get to this point, you will have made at least two other sales, as noted above. And in order to build and maintain the long-term relationships that characterize referral marketing, you have to follow up with both your new customer and your referral provider — again, part of the total sales process.

Remember, the Number One Rule in referral marketing is to make your referral provider look *GREAT*. You need to demonstrate that you know how to sell to the prospect in a way that doesn't embarrass the source of your referral — that you're going to consult with the prospect, discover his needs, offer solutions based on those needs, give him some options, and not force a sale if you know you can't provide a good solution. On the other hand, if your technique is to hold the prospect hostage at his kitchen table until he breaks down and buys, your Referral Source will not be pleased that you've abused your relationship with him and damaged his relationship with your client. You may get the deal, but you've shut yourself off from further deals with that client — and with any future referrals from your source.

— MIKE MACEDONIO

The message about sales in referral marketing is this: if you're not comfortable in making sales or if you haven't been professionally trained, sales training is an investment worth your while. It will serve you well in every facet of relationship marketing and referral networking.

⇒ Action Items

1. Measure how comfortable you are in the sales process — What professional training have you had in making sales?
2. Describe your sales process and objectives when selling yourself to a Referral Source.
3. Describe your sales process when meeting a referred prospect.
4. Communicate this sales process to your Referral Sources.

6

Networking is More About Farming Than Hunting

Cultivate Your Relationships as a Farmer Cultivates a Field

The key message of this book is that building your business through referrals is more about farming than hunting: it's about cultivating relationships with other business professionals.

Many years ago, we learned that you could have almost anything you want in business or in life — if you're willing to help other people get what *they* want. As we move further into a new century, we must look back at the enduring values that have served successful businesses well. One of these is trust. We use the services of people and businesses that we trust. Therefore, if we expect others to refer us, we must gain their trust. This is *a process* — a process of farming, of cultivating relationships that can forge long-lasting referral partnerships.

Unfortunately, in this high-tech society we tend to look for immediate results. Referral marketing is not a get-rich-quick scheme or the latest fad. It is a solid foundation upon which you can build a successful business. So, in order to benefit from this approach, you must understand that building trust takes time. With a bit of persistence, the right effort, and a little time, you can get almost 100 percent of your new business through referrals.

Now, if you're just starting to work your referral marketing plan, the idea that you could get 100 percent of your business by referral may seem like pie in the sky. But we are here to tell you that it *can* be done — it *has* been done, and *you* can do it, too.

We teach by example: several years ago, the Referral Institute put in place a referral marketing plan to expand the company through franchising. In less than five years, the organization had over 50 franchises on four continents, and *we achieved this feat 100 percent by referral*. To put that into perspective, there are over 3,000 franchised companies in the U.S., and less than 5 percent ever grow to over 50 franchised units.

Calvin Coolidge once said, "Nothing in the world can take the place of persistence. Talent will not; nothing is more common than unsuccessful men with talent. Genius will not; unrewarded genius is almost a proverb. Education will not; the world is full of educated derelicts."

Persistence and determination are the keys to success in any referral marketing effort. For example, many years ago a man failed in business. The following year, he was defeated for a seat in the legislature. The next year he failed in business again. Three years later, he suffered a nervous breakdown. Two years after that, he was defeated for the speakership of his state's legislature. Two years after that, he was defeated for elector. Within three years, he was defeated for a seat in the U.S. Congress. Five years later, he was defeated for Congress a second time. Seven years later, he was defeated for the U.S. Senate. The following year, he lost his bid to be vice president. Two years later, he was defeated for a seat in the Senate again. Two years after that, he was elected President of the United States. The man was Abraham Lincoln.

The message is this: don't give up. Building your referral business takes time, persistence, and a willingness to help others.

You now have the blueprint for building an incredibly successful referral-based business. If you put these ideas into practice, you will substantially increase your income. The question is: to what extent will you actually *put* these ideas into practice? Your referral marketing program will be whatever you make of it. But, of course, that's the way most things are in business or in life.

Take a plain $5 bar of iron and make it into horseshoes, and it will be worth around $11. Made into screwdrivers or kitchen knives, the same bar of iron may be worth $250; into needles, around $3,500; into balance springs for watches, almost $250,000! If a simple bar of iron can be worth anywhere from $5 to $250,000, there's no telling what the ideas in this book can be worth to the person who implements them!

We really appreciate this quotation of Ralph Waldo Emerson: "What lies before us and what lies behind us are very little compared to what lies within us." Building a referral-based business is all about tapping into the best that lies within us. It requires sharing, as well as caring, about those with whom we associate. As far as we're concerned, there is no better way to do business.

Referral marketing is all about relationship building in a structured and professional manner. One thing we've learned over our many years of building our businesses through referrals is this: it's not what you know, or who you know — it's how well you know them that makes the difference.

Create a powerful, diverse network of contacts, provide a positive message that is delivered effectively to people who know and trust you, and success will most certainly be yours.

7

The Power of the VCP Process®

The Three Phases of Building a Strong Networking Relationship

The key concept in referral marketing is *relationships*. The system of information, support, and referrals that you assemble will be based on your relationships with other individuals and businesses. Referral marketing works because these relationships work both ways: they benefit both parties.

A successful referral marketing plan includes many different kinds of relationships. Among the most important are those with your Referral Sources, with prospects these referral partners bring to you and with customers you recruit from the prospects. These relationships don't just spring up full-grown; they must be nurtured. As they grow, fed by mutual trust and shared benefits, they evolve through three phases: Visibility, Credibility, and Profitability. We call this evolution the *VCP Process*®.

Any successful relationship, whether personal or business, is unique to every pair of individuals, and it evolves over time. It starts out tentative, fragile, full of unfulfilled possibilities and expectations. It grows stronger with experience and familiarity. It matures into trust and commitment. The VCP Process® describes the process of creation, growth, and strengthening of both professional and personal relationships; it is useful for assessing the status of a relationship and where it fits in the process of getting referrals. It can be used to nurture the growth of an effective and rewarding relationship with a prospective friend, client, co-worker, vendor, colleague, or family member. When fully realized, such a relationship is mutually rewarding, and thus self-perpetuating.

Visibility

The first phase of growing a relationship is Visibility: you and another individual become aware of each other. In business terms, a potential source of referrals or a potential customer becomes aware of the nature of your business — perhaps because of your public relations and advertising efforts or, perhaps, through someone you both know. This person may observe you in the act of conducting business or relating with the people around you. The two of you begin to communicate and establish links, perhaps discussing a question or two over the phone about product availability. You may become personally acquainted and work on a first-name basis, but you know little about each other. A combination of many such relationships forms a casual-contact network, a sort of *de facto* association based on one or more shared interests.

The greater your Visibility:
- The more widely known you will be,
- The more information you will obtain about others,
- The more opportunities you will be exposed to, and
- The greater your chances will be of being accepted by other individuals or groups as someone they can or should refer business to!

The Visibility phase is important because it creates recognition and awareness. The greater your Visibility, the more widely known you will be, the more information you will obtain about others, the more opportunities you will be exposed to, and the greater your chances will be of being accepted by other individuals or groups as someone they can or should refer business to. Visibility must be actively maintained and developed. Without it, you cannot move on to the next level.

The litmus test to determine if you are in Visibility with a Referral Source is whether you know who they are and what they do and they know that same about you. NOTE: While going through your database, you may come across contacts that do not meet this criterion. You can refer to these contacts as being in *pre*-Visibility.

Credibility

Credibility is the quality of being reliable, or worthy of confidence. Once you and your new acquaintance begin to form expectations of each other — and if the expectations are fulfilled — your relationship can enter the Credibility stage. If each person is confident of gaining satisfaction from the relationship, then it will continue to strengthen.

Credibility grows when appointments are kept, promises are acted upon, facts are verified, and services are rendered. The old saying that results speak louder than words is true. This is very important. Failure to live up to expectations — to keep both explicit and implicit promises — can kill a budding relationship before it breaks through the ground and can create 'visibility' of a kind you don't want!

To determine how credible you are, people often turn to third parties. They ask someone they know who has known you longer or perhaps who has done business with you. Will she vouch for you? Are you honest? Are your products and services effective? Are you someone who can be counted on in a crunch?

When evaluating your VCP relationships, you will want to keep in mind that the relationship is two-sided. It is the combination of your perception and theirs reduced to the lowest common denominator. For example, if you feel as though you're in Credibility with someone but they feel you are in Visibility, you would have to conclude you are in a Visibility relationship.

Profitability

The mature relationship, whether business or personal, can be defined in terms of its Profitability. Is it mutually rewarding? Do both partners gain satisfaction from it? Does it maintain itself by providing benefits to both? If it doesn't profit both partners to keep it going, it probably will not endure.

The time it takes to pass through the phases of a developing relationship is highly variable. It's not always easy to determine when profitability has been achieved — a week? A month? One year? In a time of urgent need, you and a client may proceed from Visibility to Credibility overnight. The same is true of Profitability: it may happen quickly, or it may take years — most likely, somewhere in between. It depends on the frequency and quality of the contacts, and especially on the desire of both parties to move the relationship forward.

Shortsightedness can impede full development of the relationship. Perhaps you're a customer who has done business with a certain vendor off and on for several months, but to save pennies you keep hunting around for the lowest price, ignoring the value this vendor provides in terms of service, hours, goodwill, and reliability. Are you really profiting from the relationship, or are you stunting its growth? Perhaps if you gave this vendor all your business, you could work out terms that would benefit both of you.

Profitability is not found by bargain hunting. Recall our discussion of farming versus hunting in Chapter 6: profitability must be cultivated, and, like farming, it takes patience. Suppose you plant an apple tree in your front yard. You feed and water it, watching it grow from a sapling to a young tree. You wait for fruit to develop. After three years, no apples are visible, so you pull up the tree and move it to the backyard. The tree spends the next two years recovering from the move, and still it refuses to yield. So you move it again. As you can well imagine, this tree may never bear fruit for you — even if you don't manage to kill it.

Visibility and Credibility are important in the relationship-building stages of the referral marketing process.

The qualifier for a **Profitability referral relationship** would be some-one who proactively and consistently refers business to you, and you do the same for her. You can see by this criterion that a *Profitability referral relationship is much more than someone who has done business with you or has sent you some referrals in the past.* The good news is that most business only needs a few profitable referral relationships to be very successful.

It's important to realize that these three terms, as used here, are describ-ing the *referral* process, not a *sales* process. This can be confusing at first, and some people might mistakenly assume that just because someone bought something from them, they are in a Profitability relationship with that person. This is not the case. In this context, *you are in a Profitability relationship **ONLY IF** you are at the point where a person is referring to you on a consistent basis.*

Just as relationships can be categorized by Visibility, Credibility, and Profitability, we can also identify networking behavior with the VCP Process®. The relationship that you have with the participants at a network-ing event will play a major role on the type of networking you are doing.

For example, let's say you are at a networking event where you don't know the attendees. You start to work the room, making introductions and collecting business cards. If a week or two were to pass without mak-ing any contact, what are the chances the people you met would be able to identify you by your first name, last name, and profession? If they could not do this for you, or if you could not identify them, you would be in pre-Visibility, as we mentioned earlier in this chapter.

This can become a huge networking trap for many businesspeople. When we evaluate the networking effectiveness of business owners, we often find them investing their networking time in pre-Visibility and Visibility networking. They fall into the trap because from time to time they may run into a prospect they have met before. This in turn makes it feel as if it's working — that they are getting in front of the same people now and again, and they should continue to meet new people and network on this level. The reality is, however, that it is very unlikely that they would get referrals from people with whom they are in pre-Visibility or Visibility.

> It is very unlikely that you would get referrals from people with whom you are in pre-Visibility or Visibility.

When would you put your reputation on the line and recommend someone? Most business people tell us that they would need to believe the person to be in at least a solid Credibility stage. As a side note, this may be worth considering when it is appropriate to ask for referrals.

A common pitfall with the VCP Process® is how people will overestimate the level of relationship they are in with their Referral Relationships. One thing to keep in mind is that we are talking about the *Referral Process* when evaluating these relationships. When someone chooses to do business with you, he may have a tendency to believe this means you are in the Credibility or even the Profitability stage. Your level of relationship in the *Sales Process* may not translate in the *Referral Process*. It is possible for someone to buy from you and not be at the Credibility stage, where they would be willing to put their reputation on the line for you.

"People are more willing to open their wallets than expose their reputations."

— MIKE MACEDONIO

Here's a quiz for you: you are attending a networking event, meeting and greeting new contacts. Over the course of the evening, you collect a couple of dozen business cards. Following the event, you input your new contacts into your database so they can now start receiving your email offers or newsletter. What type of networking would you evaluate this to be: Visibility, Credibility, or Profitability networking?

Answer: None of the above! This is called *Irritability Networking.* They never asked to have their inbox filled with your emails. Remember, networking is about helping others as a way to grow your business. You can be much more successful networking when you make the effort to help them and in turn move the relationship from pre-Visibility to Visibility, then to Credibility, and then to Profitability.

> The secret to maximizing your results in less time is to re-invest your time from pre-Visibility/ Visibility networking to Credibility/Profitability networking.

The secret to maximizing your results in less time is to re-invest your time from pre-Visibility/Visibility networking to Credibility/Profitability networking.

⇒ Action Items

1. List the top 20 relationships in your referral network.
2. Without accessing your database, if you can name their first name, last name, and what they do, you can qualify them as a Visibility relationship.
3. Grade the relationship as Credibility if you can document how you have helped the person.
4. Grade the relationship as Profitability if you are proactively and consistently referring to them and they are doing the same for you.
5. Starting with your strongest relationships and working your way down the list, set up a plan to meet with everyone on your list and move them forward to the next level in the VCP Process®.

8

The Ten Commandments of Networking a Mixer

Joining the Crowd

If you've never attended a networking event, you may be a little nervous about your first experience at one. That's only natural. The room will be full of people who are mostly strangers to you, and you'll notice right away that most of them seem to know other attendees (some of them seem to be acquainted with everybody!) and will be engaged in lively conversations. Unless you're the most gregarious person on the planet, you'll have some butterflies at the idea of going in and meeting all these new people.

Although it's natural to be nervous, be assured that it would be hard to find a more open, inviting group of people than a gathering of business networkers. These are men and women who delight in meeting new people and welcoming them into their networks. Most are just naturally interested in people, and every new face represents a potential new relationship, as well as a richer personal, social, and business experience down the line.

But when you go to a mixer or other informal gathering, your first glimpse of the room may be daunting. You're confronted with a room full of strangers busily involved in conversations. If you were a fly on the chandelier, you might see something like this:

Where do I start?

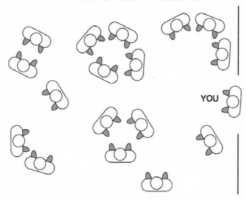

You see that conversations are going on in clusters of two, three, or four or more people. As a stranger, you may feel that if you try to join any of the clusters, you will be intruding. It's an awkward moment, and you may not know quite what to do or where to start.

But take a closer look. The clusters are different, and not just in the number of people in them. The way the groups are configured can tell you a lot about how you will be received if you approach them. Notice, for instance, that some of the groups are configured like these:

Closed Twos – Closed Threes

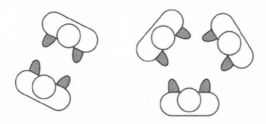

The people in these groups, a *closed* two and a *closed* three, are facing inward, away from the rest of the room. They are engaged in private conversations. No matter which direction you approach from, their backs are turned to you. These groups are closed, at least for the moment. Unless you like awkward pauses or hostile glares, don't try to force yourself in.

Other clusters will look more like these:

Open Twos – Open Threes

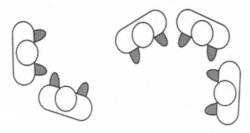

These groups, exemplified here as an *open* two and an *open* three, have left an open side from which you can approach them face-to-face. This orientation is a welcoming configuration; it signals that their conversation is not private and that you would be welcome to join them and introduce yourself.

If you watch for a few minutes, you'll see groups open and close; this is an outward sign of the ebb and flow of the conversation. When a closed group opens, it means there is a break in the intensity of the conversation, or at least in its privacy. Some of the participants may be looking around the room, getting ready either to move or to accept new people into the cluster. That's a good time to join because it often means the conversation has slowed down or come to a halt and they're ready for a fresh topic or a fresh face.

As you enter the room, here's what your awareness of these cluster dynamics should be telling you:

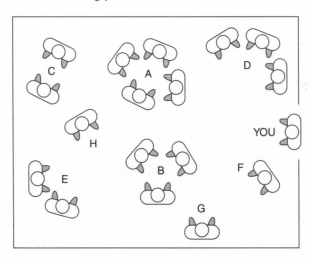

Groups that are closed, like A, B, and C, are probably engaged in private conversations and are not good places to introduce yourself, at least for the moment. Person F, who entered the room just ahead of you, is heading straight for Person G, who apparently knows him. They probably have some things to say to each other. Don't join them immediately; wait until you see whether they form an open two or a closed two.

Groups that have an open side, like D and E, are implicitly welcoming you to join them. Slide in and listen for a while until you can unobtrusively join the conversation. The others will probably smile and introduce themselves, and you will have started the process of making new friends. Person H, on the other hand, seems to be standing by himself for the moment; this might be a good opportunity to walk up and immediately introduce yourself.

Some of the people who attend a mixer will stay grouped together for the entire event. However, if you watch these fixed groups closely, you will see that they open and close from time to time, as noted earlier. Other groups will break up and reform in different combinations. Watch and be ready to move to a new open group or to introduce yourself to new people who join the group you're in. You will soon get the feel of the room and will be comfortable navigating from one group to another. Before long the new person coming through the door will see you and think you are the most popular networker in the room.

Learning how to read a crowd, whatever its size, and gauge when to join a group of people who are networking, is an acquired skill. Without it, you might find such gatherings daunting and, after unsuccessfully wandering through a few, decide that networking events are not your game.

Nothing could be further from the truth. Networking is a contact sport. You've got to put yourself out there, get into the mix, to become a good networker. In order to make those connections, you need to be able to gauge the warmth of the groups you see at a mixer.

It's still a long journey from 'fresh face' to 'master networker,' but being able to read a room will certainly get you through that daunting first meeting. You may even find it so enjoyable that you'll not only be ready, but also eager to show up at the next one!

Now it's time to get out there and network a mixer!

Getting the Most from Casual Contacts

Making contacts that turn into relationships is the foundation of a prosperous referral-based business. Neophyte networkers repeatedly ask, "What can I do to meet more people and make better contacts at business mixers?" To answer this important question, Ivan has put together what he calls the "Ten Commandments of Networking a Mixer." These rules work just as well for events like a Chamber of Commerce mixer as a company open-house party.

By their nature, mixers present Casual Contact opportunities, which we will be talking about later.

Commandment 1:
Have Your Networking Tools with You at All Times

The first of the Ten Commandments is to have the tools you need to network with you *at all times*. This is the foundation of all that follows. All successful business people have the 'tools of the trade.' Notable Networkers' tools include an informative name badge, plenty of business cards, brochures about their business, and a pocket-sized business-card file that has the business cards of the professionals they refer.

As an effective networker, you need to purchase a commercially made badge. These look more professional than the stick-on, "Hello My Name Is" paper badges. Your badge needs to include both your name and your company's name or your profession on it. As a rule of thumb, use your company's name if it describes your profession. For example:

> **John Anderson**
> *"Ready-Fast"*
> *Print & Copy*

If your company's name does not clearly describe your profession (as is the case with a consulting firm like Carlton, Donner, & Finch), write your profession on the badge:

> ***Mary S. Carlton***
> Advertising &
> Marketing Consultant

Badges are now available that require only slipping your business card into the top and — *voilà!* — instant badge! These badges are unique because you are literally wearing your business card, logo and all.

Make sure the print on your card is readable to people standing a few feet away. Many people recommend wearing your badge on the right side because people shake right-handed and the badge is easier to see. While this seems to makes sense, when you're that close to someone it doesn't matter much. Always look for a profession on the badge. Knowing someone's profession or company name makes it easier to start a dialogue because you can ask about his or her business. Always carry plenty of business cards with you. Stash some in your wallet, briefcase, calendar, and car so that you're never without them. We also recommend you keep a small metal cardholder in the coat pocket of each of your suits.

Commandment 2:
Set a Goal for the Number of People You'll Meet

Some people go to a meeting with only one goal in mind: the time they plan to leave! To get the most out of a networking event, set a goal regarding the number of contacts you want to make or the number of business cards you want to collect. Don't leave until you've met your goal.

If you feel inspired, set a goal to meet fifteen to twenty people and make sure you get all their cards. If you don't feel so hot, shoot for less. In either case, set a reachable goal based on the attendance and type of group.

Commandment 3:
Act Like a Host, Not a Guest

In her book, *Skills for Success,* Dr. Adele Scheele tells about a cocktail party where she met someone who was hesitant to introduce himself to total strangers. Dr. Scheele suggested that he "consider a different scenario for the evening. That is, consider himself the party's host instead of its guest." She asked him, if he were the host, wouldn't he introduce himself to people he didn't know and then introduce them to each other? Wouldn't he make sure people knew where the food and drinks were? Wouldn't he watch for lulls in conversations, or bring new people over to an already-formed small group?

Scheele's new acquaintance acknowledged the obvious difference between the active role of the host and the passive role of the guest. A host is expected to do things for others, while a guest sits back and relaxes. Scheele concluded, "There was nothing to stop this man from playing the role of host even though he wasn't the actual host." There is nothing to stop you from being far more active when you're with a large group of people, either.

Along this line, we recommend that you volunteer to be an Ambassador, or Visitor Host, at the networking groups you belong to. An Ambassador or Visitor Host is someone who greets all the visitors and introduces them to others. If you see visitors sitting, introduce yourself and ask if they would like to meet other members.

If there are many other visitors to meet, ask another member to help you by introducing the visitor to the rest of the membership so that you can get back to meeting new visitors. By using this technique, you'll start to develop excellent networking skills and get great exposure to many business professionals in a short time.

A distinguishing characteristic of self-made millionaires, according to Thomas Stanley, professor of marketing at Georgia State University, is that they network everywhere. Most important, they do it all the time — at business conferences, at the health club, on the golf course, or with the person sitting next to them on a plane. This fact alone should motivate you to place yourself in situations where you can meet new people.

Sit between strangers at business meetings or strike up a conversation with people at the spa. Make friends, even when you don't need to.

Commandment 4:
Listen, and Ask the Five "W" Questions:
Who, What, Where, When, and Why

As Dale Carnegie advised, show genuine interest in the other person's business. If you meet a printer, ask, "What kind of printing do you specialize in? Commercial? Four-color? Instant? Copying? Where are you located? How long have you been in business?"

The answer to each of these questions gives you a better grasp of the individual and the type of work she does. Thus, you're in a better position to refer her to others or invite her to different networking groups.

Commandment 5:
Give a Referral Whenever Possible

Notable Networkers believe in the Givers Gain philosophy. If you don't genuinely attempt to help the people you meet, then you are not networking. You need to be creative in this area.

Few of the people you meet for the first time at a business mixer are going to express a need for your product or service. That doesn't mean you can't give them something.

When you do meet someone that expresses a need, and you know someone that can satisfy that need, take advantage of the opportunity to recommend to people in your network that can help them. Please do not misinterpret this to mean that we are saying you should be trying to refer business to someone you just met. It would be dangerous to recommend someone with whom you are barely in Visibility (see Chapter 7). You will be referring your new contact to someone already in your network that you know and trust.

If you work hard at developing your skills, people will remember you in a positive way.

The larger your network, the better your chances of reaching out and calling upon resources you wouldn't have access to otherwise. Most important, with this growth comes increased visibility, exposure, opportunity, and success.

Commandment 6:
Describe Your Product or Service

After you've learned what other people do, make sure to tell them what you do. Be specific but brief: use a 'sharpshooter' approach and avoid telling about everything you do. Whatever you do, don't assume they know your business. Explain it to them if they seem interested. We will discuss this in more detail in the upcoming chapters.

Here is an example of a brief description that Mike uses when introducing himself as part of the Referral Institute: "I help business owners work less, play more, and double their income by creating Referrals For Life®."

Commandment 7:
Exchange Business Cards with the People You Meet

Ask the person you've just met for two of his cards, one to pass on to some-one else and one to keep for yourself. This sets the stage for networking to happen. Keep your cards in one pocket and put other people's cards in the other pocket. This way, you won't be fumbling around trying to find your cards while accidentally giving away somebody else's card. What do you do with business cards you collect from people you meet at networking events such as business forums, breakfasts, and mixers? These cards can be instrumental in helping you remember people, initiate follow-ups, dis-cover opportunities, and access information and resources.

Always review the cards for pertinent information. It is not always easy to determine what people do simply from their title or company name. Note whether the products and services offered by the company are listed or summarized. If you've just received the card of an attorney, check to see whether the card indicates the attorney's specialty. To demonstrate your interest, write the missing information you collect on the front of the card, in view of the other person.

Commandment 8:
Spend Ten Minutes or Less with Each Person
You Meet and Don't Linger with Friends and Associates

Recalling Commandment 2, if your goal is to meet a given number of people, then you can't spend too much time with any one person, no mat-ter how interesting the conversation gets. Stay focused on making as many contacts as you can. When you meet people who are very interesting and with whom you want to spend more time, set up appointments with them. You can always meet later to continue the conversation.

Don't try to close business deals while you're networking — it's imprac-tical. Set a date to meet and discuss your product or service in an envi-ronment more conducive to doing business. You may be able to increase your business with hot prospects if you take the time to fully understand their needs.

Learn to leave conversations gracefully. Honesty is usually the best policy: tell them you need to connect with a few more people, sample the hors d'oeuvres, or get another drink. If you feel uncomfortable with that, exit like a host by introducing new acquaintances to someone you know. Better yet, if it seems appropriate, ask them to introduce you to people they know.

Above all, don't linger with friends and associates! These are people you already know, and you're there to meet people you don't know. Ivan attended a mixer once where he saw several business friends stand and talk with one another for two hours. On their way out, one actually complained, "This was a waste of time. I didn't get any business from it, did you?" No kidding.

Commandment 9:
Write Comments on the Backs of the Business Cards You Collect

This helps you remember more about the person when you follow up the next day. You can benefit from Ivan's personal experience:

I try to meet many people when I'm at a mixer. Two hours and twenty people later, I can't always keep everyone straight. Therefore, I always carry a pen, and when I've concluded a conversation with a new acquaintance, I step away and jot down notes, including the date and location of the event. This information is crucial for effective follow-up and becomes more important the busier you are. I also write a note about what the person is seeking. For example:

"*. . . wants to visit BNI,*"
"*. . . looking for a good printer,*"
"*. . . has friend moving out of the area and needs a real-estate agent,*" *or the most important one of all,*
"*. . . wants to set an appointment with me; call on Tuesday.*"

If the individual doesn't express a specific need, I may write down something about him or her that I learned from the conversation, things relating to his or her responsibilities, contacts, interests, or hobbies. For example:

"*. . . likes to back-pack,*"
"*. . knows Joe Smith from L.A.,*" *or*
"*. . . supervises ten employees.*"

Record anything you think may be useful in remembering the person more clearly. As you'll see in Commandment 10, the more information you have about the people you meet, the better your chances of a successful follow-up.

Business Card Etiquette in Asia:

Exchanging business cards is an essential part of most cultures. In most Asian countries, after a person has introduced him or herself and bowed, the business card ceremony begins. In Japan, this is called *meishi*. The card is presented to the other person with the front side facing upwards toward the recipient. Offering the card with both hands holding the top corners of the card demonstrates respect for the other person.

The business card is much more in the Asian culture than it is to us here in America. It is truly an extension of the individual and is treated with respect. Things like tucking it into a pocket after receiving it, writing on it, bending or folding it in any way, or even looking at it again after you have first accepted it and looked at it, are not considered polite and can insult your fellow Asian networker.

Commandment 10:
Follow Up with the People You Meet

We've seen people spend untold hours in networking organizations, yet fail at networking because their follow-up was appalling. Remember, good follow-up is the lifeblood of networking. You can obey the previous nine commandments religiously, but if you don't follow up effectively, you're wasting your time!

If you promise to get back to people, make sure you do. Even if you don't promise, call them or drop them a letter. Your follow-up can include an invitation to receive your newsletter; however, you don't want your new contact to start receiving what they perceive to be spam. If you follow up effectively, networking can be empowering.

The next time you have the opportunity to go to a gathering of professionals in a networking setting, keep the Ten Commandments of Networking a Mixer in mind. We highly recommend that you keep a copy of this list of commandments and keep it with you in your day planner, briefcase, or purse. The next time you go to a business mixer, review the list before you go inside.

This chapter is part of the core of creating a positive message and delivering it effectively. Establishing a referral-based business requires 'getting out of your cave' (see Chapter 15, "Cave Dwellers") and getting belly-to-belly with other business professionals.

⇒ *Action Items*

1. Purchase a commercially made badge, and always bring plenty of business cards.
2. To get the most out of a networking event, set a goal for the number of contacts you will make, or the number of business cards you want to collect. Don't leave until you've met your goal.
3. Act like a host, not a guest. There's nothing to stop you from being far more active when you're with a large group of people. Volunteer to be a Visitor Host at the networking groups you belong to.
4. Keep asking questions about what the other person does.
5. If you can't refer people to others that can help them, offer other information that would be of interest to them.
6. After you've learned what the other person does, make sure to tell him or her what you do. Be specific but brief.
7. Exchange business cards with the people you meet.
8. Stay focused on making as many contacts as you can — Don't linger with friends and associates! Don't try to close business deals while you're networking: it's impractical.
9. Write comments on the business cards you collect. Good follow-up is the lifeblood of networking. If you promise to get back to someone, make sure you do it.

9

Making Introductions That Last

Make Meaningful Contact

Your primary goal in building a referral-based business is to increase the amount of business you get. To do this, you must make meaningful contact with other business professionals who can either use your services, refer someone else who can use your services, or both. Thus, referral marketing is a team sport.

Stand and Deliver

Whether you're introducing yourself to an individual or to a group, you have a choice of how you deliver your message. The primary vehicle for your introduction is your verbal presentation. Does your introduction work?

People will judge not only the message, but the messenger as well. How you look, carry yourself, listen, and leave the conversation will affect what others do with the message you've delivered. The important thing to remember is to speak as if you're addressing a single person, a good friend.

Small Talk vs. Smart Talk

Serious networkers, recognizing that they have limited time to introduce themselves and convey the essence of what they do, generally avoid lengthy small talk.

If you want to build your business through referrals, you must give a message that's fully heard by others. Take the time to plan your introduction and prepare some concise and descriptive overviews of your products or services. Then, when you meet someone for the first time, you can give him a good explanation of what you have to offer. We recommend that you develop several scripts that you can readily use when attending networking meetings.

Brief Introductions

When participating in various business organizations, even as a guest, you will be required to introduce yourself. Preparing a script for introducing yourself will improve your results. One of your scripts should be an overview of what you do. Other presentations can address various aspects of your product or service. Here's the recommended sequence for a script for first time introductions:

- Your name
- Your business or profession
- A benefit statement of one of your products or services (what you do that helps others)
- Your name, again

Stating your name and your business or profession is easy enough. A brief description and the benefit statement can be separate items, but more often they are intertwined in your message. For example, it's easy to combine your business with the benefits of your product or service. We suggest telling people what you do, as well as what you are:

"I'm a financial planner, and I help people plan for their future."

"I'm an advertising and marketing consultant: I help companies get the most out of their advertising dollar."

These explanations are more effective than saying, "I do financial planning" or "I plan advertising campaigns."

Moving Beyond the "First Time" Introduction

It's important to emphasize that the above script is recommended for *first time* introductions. Some networking organizations meet weekly and have all the members take turns standing at each meeting and, in round-robin fashion, give a one-minute overview to the entire group at each meeting. If you're a member of a group like this, it is vitally important to vary your presentations.

Many people who are in business groups that meet every week have a tendency to say the same old thing, time after time. From what we've seen, many weekly presentations are also *'weakly done'* presentations! Uninteresting, unvarying, repetitive presentations are weak presentations. If yours is like this, many people will tune you out when you speak because they've already heard your message several times. Your best bet is to give a brief overview and then concentrate on just one element of your business for the rest of your presentation.

After you become more experienced and confident in presenting yourself, it's time to take a look at how to stand out and produce results. At any given event, the audience is constantly being distracted. They are being distracted by what's going on in the room or what's going on in their head (trying to figure out what they are going to say). Your challenge is to interrupt the distractions and get their attention.

Rather than starting out with saying your name, replace it with a question. The chances are everyone else in the room has been introducing themselves by starting with their name. As this is repeated, more participants start tuning out. The use of a question is a tactic to engage their minds.

One of our favorite questions starts with, "Who do you know who . . .?" which is a tactic recommended by Mark Sheer, a well-known author and coach. Following the "Who do you know who . . ." would be a specific circumstance a person would be in. This is a great technique to help people identify good referrals for you. It's very powerful because it eliminates the message of "You should buy from me . . ." and teaches people to think about people they know instead.

At the same time, people will self-qualify if they fall into that situation. For example, say you are a realtor. You could ask the group: "Who do you know who just had a baby?" You could then talk about how these people may want to talk with you about the need for more space. By the same token, if you are a financial planner, you could talk about their new needs for life insurance or investing in a college plan.

Once you have engaged them with a question, the next step is to show them how you can benefit that person with your service. One of the best ways to do this is to tell a story or give a testimonial of someone you have helped in this situation.

Your next step is a call to action. We suggest using the following opening: "I can use your help with . . ." For some entrepreneurs, literally hardwired to be completely self-sufficient, these can be difficult words to get out, but they work:

- I can use your help with an introduction to Mrs. Smith.
- I can use your help getting a speaking engagement at the XYZ organization.
- I can use your help with introductions to these types of business owners.
- Now that you have their attention, you can close with your name, company, and tag line.

The following is an example of an effective 60-second presentation that Mike Macedonio has used to promote the Referral Institute. The presentation starts by the presenter standing in silence. (Three to five seconds of silence can be a great way to get your audiences' attention!) After this, Mike begins:

"Who do you know who believes that their customers are the best source of referrals? The bad news, according to the book *Truth or Delusion: Busting Networking's Biggest Myths* by Dr. Ivan Misner, is that this may not be the case. Now, the *really* bad news is that these same business owners may not know that there are seven other sources of referrals — and these sources are a lot more effective than relying only on existing customers for referrals.

"For example, I was recently working with a 10-year financial planning veteran with an extensive database of clients. After working with us, he found that he was able to develop a single Referral Source that generated more referrals than ALL of his client referrals combined.

"I could use your help getting speaking engagements with financial planners who want to learn about the seven sources of referrals other than clients.

"My name is Mike Macedonio with the Referral Institute, and I help business people create Referrals For Life®."

Memory Hooks

"Memory hooks" can be excellent tools to use when making a presentation to a new audience. A memory hook is something in your presentation that so vividly describes what you do that a person will be able to visualize it clearly in her mind's eye. This visualization of your product or service makes it easier for people to remember you whenever they meet someone who needs your service.

A memory hook would be appropriately used with a group of people you don't know at all or who may be in the early stages of the VCP Process® (introduced in Chapter 7). We are pointing this out because we have seen memory hooks overused in many referral-networking groups. The structure of a referral networking group is to meet frequently and build long-term relationships. These groups tend to have many Credibility and Profitability relationships because members see each other on such a regular basis.

Memory Hook A memory hook is something in your presentation that so vividly describes what you do that a person will be able to visualize it clearly in her mind's eye. This visualization of your product or service makes it easier for people to remember you whenever they meet someone who needs your service.

A memory hook would be appropriately used with a group of people you don't know at all, or who may be in the early stages of the VCP Process®.

The memory hook is most properly used in the pre-Visibility stage, when you may need some additional tools to help people you've just met to remember you.

If you are in a pre-Visibility networking situation, here are some notable memory hooks we've had the privilege of being 'hooked' with over the years:

- Chiropractor: "You'll feel fine when your spine's in line." Or "We're always glad to see you're back."
- Dentist: "We cater to cowards." Or "My filling station is downtown, where I put the bite on decay."
- Fitness instructor: "If you wear out your body, where are you going to live?"
- Hairdresser: "If your hair is not becoming to you, then you should be coming to me."
- Insurance Agent: "If you drive it, live in it, or work at it, we can insure it!"
- Lawyer: "Before you turn to dust, see me for your will or trust."
- Plumber: "Remember, a flush is always better than a full house."
- Realtor: "I help people find a home — not a house, but a home. Not a place where you live, but a place where you love to live."
- Roofer: "A roof done right is watertight, but a roof done wrong won't last too long!"
- Therapist: "I have the owner's manual for your mind."

As you can see, these memory hooks can really catch your audiences' attention. However, it's important to emphasis again that we have also seen the misuse and overuse of memory hooks. Your memory hook needs to be consistent with what you do and how you do it. Trying to be funny or clever when you are in a serious profession can sometimes undermine your credibility.

The use of a memory hook can be effective as part of an introduction to people you don't know. It is *not* appropriate to use the memory hook over and over with people with whom you are already in a networking relationship! As we have already mentioned briefly, *if you are in a Credibility or Profitability phase, using a memory hook is almost a complete waste of time.* The relationships in a Close Contact network like BNI are beyond the pre-Visibility stage and are not appropriate for using a memory hook.

Sharpshooter vs. Shotgun

By breaking your product or service down to its most basic form, the essence of the Sharpshooter approach (as opposed to the Shotgun approach, where you describe your business in the broadest way possible, hoping something will resonate with your prospects), you will be able to effectively describe to other people the type of work you do. What is most specific about what you do? This can be counterintuitive, such as turning your vehicle into a skid. The truth is, it is highly effective.

You have several choices of what to target with the Sharpshooter approach:

- a specific product or service
- a selected target market
- benefits unique to a particular group
- a specific situation that would qualify as a referral for you
- It is not necessary to include all four points. Any one point will achieve your objective.

Collateral Material

Use visuals whenever possible. The more things people can see, hear, feel, and touch, the more likely they are to remember your message. The more they remember, the more likely they are to refer you to other people. We are not saying you need to litter the room with brochures. As a matter of fact, in some meeting environments passing out material can be disruptive to the next speaker.

As you make presentations, always consider the needs of your audience and limit your discussion primarily to those areas. If you're giving a short presentation to a large group, focus on the part of your business you think will benefit most of the group. If you're talking to only one or two people, find out as much as you can about them.

Make No Assumptions

Many people make the fatal mistake of assuming that others know a lot about their business. We heard a florist tell a networking group, "I'm not sure what else to say. You all know what a florist does, right?" Wrong! We didn't know the variety of services and products this florist provided. He knew his business and assumed that everyone else knew it as well. Later, we asked him whether his shop was an FTD florist, and —

- Did he accept credit cards?
- Did he offer seasonal specials for holidays? If so, which ones?
- Did he handle emergency orders?
- Could he do weddings?
- Did he give a discount to members?
- Could customers set up a billing arrangement with his company?
- Did he have an 800 number?
- Could customers order by fax?
- Do certain colors of roses signify certain things?
- What type of arrangement was appropriate for a graduation?
- Could he give me any tips on keeping flowers alive longer?
- What was his most challenging order?

There were hundreds of things we didn't know about his business. He lost a golden opportunity by not using his time before the group to tell everyone something special or unique about his service.

Everyone has something to say about their businesses that will educate people about the services they have to offer. Keep this in mind, and don't pass up a chance to teach people more about what *you* do!

Preparing for Your Presentation

Preparing an effective, brief introduction can usually be done without a lot of effort. First, write out your presentation and refine what you've written, several times if necessary. Next, practice your presentation on someone you know before using it at your next networking group. When your test audience understands what you have to offer and likes the way you present it, you're ready for larger arenas.

It is impossible to have a positive message, delivered effectively, if you don't prepare presentations and practice them before introducing them to your fellow networkers!

Show Pride in Who You Are and What You Do

It doesn't matter what station you have reached in life: you should always take pride in where you are at that moment. For instance, when Martha Taft was a young girl in elementary school, she was asked to introduce herself to a group of people. "My name is Martha Bowers Taft," said the child. "My great-grandfather was President of the United States. My grandfather was a United States Senator. My daddy is Ambassador to Ireland. And I am a Brownie."

⇒ *Action Items*

Create a 60-second presentation about your business or profession, following these guidelines:

1. Keep in mind that your message is to teach other business people who you are and how to refer you.
2. Open with a question such as, "Who do you know who . . . ? or "Did you know . . . ?" and give a specific description of the person or situation you are looking for.
3. Explain how your business can help that circumstance. Tell a story or give a testimonial of someone you have helped.
4. Have a call to action. "I can use your help with an introduction to . . . (be laser specific) . . . for the opportunity to . . ."
5. Close with your name, company, and benefit statement.

10

Communicating Your Brand

Tools and Techniques to Enhance Your Business Image

Image

A very important part of creating a positive message, delivered effectively, is deciding what you're going to be, what you're going to offer, and who you're going to offer it to. Let's explore how to create an image that will work for you around the clock.

According to Jeff Davidson, author of *Marketing on a Shoestring*: "The age of image is here. From corporations to individuals, the impact of image is irrefutable." We show our desire for image enhancement on many levels: seminars on grooming, speaking, interpersonal communications, negotiations, video appearances, and wardrobe management are thriving.

Why is this? Because we are constantly bombarded with information and images through our daily work, travel, and television, and our minds have learned to assimilate these stimuli quickly. We make snap judgments — correctly or incorrectly — and move on. Because of this, we agree with this point, also by Jeff Davidson: "The success of your business, whether large or small, often depends upon how you position yourself and what you project."

Your Business Image and How To Enhance It

For this chapter, we consulted with our Referral Institute partner, Eddie Esposito, from New Orleans. Eddie is a long-time business coach, an expert in referral marketing, and has helped many business owners and entrepreneurs to create effective referral marketing plans. As Eddie states, "An important part of any marketing plan is to project and maintain the company image in everything you do."

According to Entrepreneur.com's online encyclopedia of terms, *business image* is defined as: *The perception people have of your business when they hear your company name. A business's image is composed of an infinite variety of facts, events, personal histories, advertising, and goals that work together to make an impression on the public.*

If you really look at that statement, you can easily see that since it's an "infinite" collection of events and history, everything we do either adds or subtracts from our business image. That thought can be pretty intimidating, but in reality it can also serve as a guideline that holds you accountable to that image. All your activities, the products you supply, and the people you have around you, must live up to that image in order to maintain it.

Image is important because it is often the basis for making decisions. Those decisions can be for purchasing your product or service, loaning you money, or deciding whether or not to become referral partners with you. As an example, how many times have you researched a product and bought from the place where you felt most comfortable, that portrayed what you wanted or expected to see, even if the other place was less expensive?

Your stakeholders are the segments of the public you should take into consideration for your image. A stakeholder is any individual or organization that is affected by the activities of a business. They may have a direct or indirect interest in the business, and may be in contact with the business on a daily basis or just occasionally.

Essentially, you want your image to carry over to your family and friends, neighbors, bankers, target market, vendors, and anyone that you come into contact with. While the temptation may be to focus solely on your target market, you must remember you are working on a networking and referral marketing plan. All of the people mentioned above are in your network, and your image must carry on consistently throughout the entire network.

To further make our point, we asked Eddie to come up with some essential elements to project a 'round-the-clock' image of you and your company. After doing some research and collaborating with New Orleans Public Relations expert Jennifer Kelly, Eddie developed a list of 10 essential elements for any business owner or entrepreneur to be successful for projecting and maintaining a positive business image:

1. **Have Well-Crafted Mission and Vision Statements**
   The first order of business in creating a positive image is deciding what you're going to be, what you're going to offer, and who

you're going to offer it to. This begins with well-crafted vision and mission statements. It's from these statements that the image of the business begins to take shape. The statements define what the company will look like, how it will act based on its values, and its business purpose. For example, if in your company's vision and mission statements it is clear you are trying to establish yourself as a premier fitness company that values exercise and nutrition, then as a minimum we would expect — and draw a picture of this in our minds — trainers in top physical condition, state of the art equipment, and healthy meals in its restaurant.

2. **Establish an Appropriate Look**

   The look of your business begins with your logo. This is an area where strong consideration should be given to hiring a professional. A professionally designed logo that successfully conveys the image you are trying to promote to your stakeholders is a fundamental element in creating a positive business image. Your logo will be seen on everything from your business card to your brochure/letterhead to your website, so it's important to have one that captures the essence of your company and personifies your mission and vision statements. It should incorporate the style and colors used to create an image in the minds of your stakeholders (clients, prospects, referral partners, etc.) that matches the image you are working to project.

3. **Plan Your Telephone Strategy**

   Having a dedicated business line, answered promptly and appropriately, goes a long way towards establishing a positive business image. Other things to consider about your business phone and upholding your image are as follows:

   o Who answers your business phone, a person or a machine?
   o When customers are on hold, is there a message playing that can help you take advantage of the captive audience, or are they sitting in unending silence?
   o Is the phone number listed in conventional and Internet listings so you are easy to find?

   Having a good telephone setup helps project legitimacy.

4. **Facility**

While the telephone, email, and blogs are often used to project your image, they are somewhat anonymous. Realistically, you could be sitting in a hot tub while talking on the phone or writing a blog. But if you do have a storefront or place of business, when someone visits you in your facility, everything is there in the open for all to see, so —

o Does your facility live up to the image you are trying to project?
o Do the people that work there, the things hanging on the wall, the organization, style, and colors project what you want?
o Is it properly equipped?

Think about what you expect in an accountant's office compared to what you expect from a graphic designer's office. While you might expect both to be organized and properly equipped, you probably wouldn't think twice if the graphic designer's office was whimsical, brightly colored with all kinds of fun stuff on display. However, you would probably expect a little more serious tone from your accountant.

5. **Email**

Since email has become the preferred way for businesses to communicate, it is important to consider how this method of communication can affect your image. To begin, do you have an email address and domain name for the company? An instant bad hit on your image is to send out emails for company business from an address that doesn't include your company web domain. If you get an email from rod55@freemail.com, what image do you take away from that initial contact? Secondly, email templates are easy to set up and can contain your photo and logo, allowing you to keep that look consistent throughout your communication. Finally, be sure to watch what you send out and the language you use in email. Emails are easily forwarded, and you never know who may eventually see your email. For this reason, you should treat every business email as you would any other written communication: it should be well written, to the point, and free from grammatical errors!

6. **Coordinate Your Collateral Materials**

You should begin your collateral materials with professionally designed business cards that are an extension of the image that was developed with the mission and vision statements, and —

o When you hand them out, are they crisp and clean?
o Are your stationary, envelopes, and thank you notes consistent with your look?
o Are the colors, logo, and feel coordinated?
o Are your brochures informative and professionally designed?
o Do they maintain the look you established?
o Are they professionally printed and folded?

7. **Have a Great Website**

In today's business world, a website is no longer an option, it's an absolute necessity. It is likely that customers, vendors, potential referral partners, and other stakeholders will visit your website well before they ever call or meet you. Additionally, if someone has been referred to you, this is often the first place they will look to find out about you. Websites today need to be informative, clear, and easy to find. Be sure to have your site professionally designed, consistent with the look you have established, and search engine optimized. Another key element is easy navigation. Plan with your designer or Webmaster to have important content available in 2-3 clicks. Also, don't forget your social media accounts. For example, if you have a business page on Facebook or a Twitter account, make sure they include your logo and that all written content, images, and photos are consistent with your overall brand.

8. **Manage Yourself**

What is the professional standard expected by your stakeholders of you and your profession? Do you and your staff live up to it consistently? Every person in the organization has to dress and act appropriately to uphold the image of the company. While the delivery drivers for a catering company may not need to wear a business suit, it upholds the image of the company if they are dressed in clothes that match the look established for the company. This includes colors, logo, and style. Don't leave the interpretation of what upholds your image up to the staff. Remain consistent in your decisions for dress, and consider uniforms or items with logos to help reinforce your image

9. **Understand the Importance of Your Vehicles**

   If your clients or prospects are going to see you or your employees in the act of driving a vehicle, the type of vehicle used for this purpose matters. Even if you can't have a new car, be sure the one you do have is neat and well kept. If you are projecting the image of a successful business advisor, that image may take a hit in the eyes of your client if you drive up in an old clunker! Likewise, if your delivery vehicles are beat up and dirty, that won't do a whole lot to help promote the image of your catering company. On one of Eddie's trips, he was picked up from the airport by a taxi that was spotless, had that day's newspaper in the back, and the driver offered him a drink from a small cooler he had in front. This driver certainly had a good handle on projecting his image, even though his car wasn't new.

10. **Manage your Social Networking**

    As we mentioned in number 7, above, social networking sites have become very popular and useful tools. However, we cannot stress enough that everything posted on the Internet is an extension of your company's image. Make wise decisions, and if you have a staff, consider implementing a social media policy for your company. If you don't feel comfortable in the social media arena, consider working with a marketing or public relations specialist to assist you.

Everything you produce, sell, give away, write, and say contributes to the creation of your image in the minds of your stakeholders. Be vigilant about your image, and don't hesitate to hire professionals to create and produce the materials you need to ensure consistency.

Using Public Relations to Build Your Image

Another important aspect of a great referral marketing plan is an appropriate public relations (PR) strategy. In our media-oriented society, your survival and growth in business are often based on how you appear in the media, whether in print, on television, or online. Pick up your area's business magazines or the business section of the daily newspaper or website.

Every issue of these publications carries an interview or feature on a corporate executive or local entrepreneur.

Public relations firms that are paid by the subject of the story place most of them. The profiles you see are part of a coordinated effort undertaken and funded by the company or individual being publicized. The people or companies being featured are paying for it, or sometimes generating it themselves with concerted in-house PR effort.

Suppose you're a remodeling subcontractor in Spokane and the city council has voted to restore an historic building. One well-placed interview on the significance of this structure to the community is likely to catch the eye of hundreds of builders and developers, preservation groups, historical societies, and anyone else concerned with architecture or historic preservation.

We know of a Richmond, Virginia-based hardware store owner who wanted to increase his visibility in the community and attract new business. To highlight and promote his line of products, he announced that he would sponsor an urban sculpture contest, in which participants must use only junk hardware parts. He had 'in progress' and 'completion' photos taken to illustrate the efforts of the participants. He also hired a PR agent from the very beginning of the contest to ensure maximum exposure. A few weeks after the entries were judged, a major story appeared in one of the region's most prestigious monthly magazines. The public relations agent prepared communications, distributed the pitch, and solicited the magazine to run the story under the by-line of the publicity agent.

To the average reader — indeed, even to the average marketer — it appeared that the publication either contracted with the writer to produce this story or accepted the piece as written by an outside agent.

Public Relations: Different from Advertising

The cost of getting an article about you or your business written and published, which may span several pages and include photos, is likely to be far less than the cost of a single-page ad in the same publication. Think of PR vs. advertising as *earned* media vs. *paid* media. The difference is you are usually not guaranteed to get the article or interview, while a paid advertisement is guaranteed to appear, according to a contract. While the advanced planning, coordination, and acceptance of a self-generated article requires some effort, it is often a sound investment. Even if targets don't see the article when it first runs, you can make attractive reprints on high-quality, glossy stock and use them for several years as key items in your arsenal of collateral materials!

To Get Your Business in the News You Must Be Newsworthy

Surprisingly, editors and reporters need story ideas from wherever they can find them. Too many people who seek to be featured in newspapers or magazines send company brochures rather than a news release. They fail to realize that editors and reporters need hooks, angles, and ways to relate to a distracted, overworked, frenzied readership. Do your homework — Sending the right story to the wrong reporter wastes everyone's time.

Many newspapers and local journals are interested in receiving articles that will add interest to their pages. Inform the editor why readers will be interested in the feature idea you have, or why it is newsworthy. What are you doing in your business that strikes a chord in the community? What are the broad ramifications?

Can you prime the pump with editors and reporters? Certainly. Read the publications you'd like to be in, and find the reporter covering your topic of interest. Then email or call with your best story idea. When you call, be as professional with the reporter or editor as you are with everyone else.

Consider all media for your message, but make sure the audience is a match for your company. All media can provide some demographic data about their audience. As with maintaining your business image, if you really want to institute a consistent PR campaign, consider hiring a professional to help you develop a plan.

10 Ways To Generate PR for Your Business

We have compiled the list below as an at-a-glance tool for you to start and build your PR strategy:

1. Write an Article

You can create or enhance your identity and credibility by addressing issues of importance to the people you wish to serve. One of the best ways to do that is to write an article on the subject. If you don't feel your writing skills are up to snuff, hire a professional writer to put your idea into an acceptable form for publishing.

Simply getting into print establishes your credibility and improves your visibility by reaching thousands of prospects in one effort. By inference, people will assume that a prestigious media outlet thinks enough of you and your message to print it, which is a tacit endorsement of your expertise.

You can identify potential markets for your article by going to the library and looking through *Writer's Market*, the recognized leader in where and how to sell your articles to periodicals of all kinds.

You need to be aware that you may not get paid directly for your effort. Editors may consider printing your article as payment enough for the exposure you'll receive. Sometimes an editor will print your article in exchange for advertising space. Also remember that if you are paid for your article, the publication owns it. You may want to work out a deal if you want to use reprints in your other marketing materials.

Even if a publisher doesn't accept your article, you can still use it as part of your overall marketing strategy.

2. Write a Column

"Prestige and professional enhancement are easy to attain. You could gain local, regional, and even national exposure by writing a column," says author Charlotte Degregorio, author of *You Can Be a Columnist*. You can contact a local publication and pitch the idea of regularly published content on a subject that will build your image in the community.

The opportunities for having a column published are greater than you may think. There are almost 1,400 newspapers across the United States. While you may not be able to interest the *New York Times* in a column, you might be able to convince a regional or local paper that your expertise could benefit its readers. Go around town and collect all of the free community newspapers, quarterlies, and bimonthlies you can find, and check out their contents. Choose a few that seem to speak to a readership that would be a good match with your target market. Then call the editor and pitch him on an idea for your column. If you get an offer, go out and buy a copy of *You Can Be a Columnist*, and you're in business.

3. Publish a Newsletter

Publishing a newsletter can be an effective means for developing name and brand recognition. Newsletters allow you to tell people who you are and what products or services you provide. They also build awareness in the market place and contribute to building your reputation as a credible expert in your field. Sending them by email also keeps costs down.

There are many kinds of newsletters. The design and length of yours is determined by how much work you want to put into it, how often you want to publish it, and how much you want to spend on it.

Publishing a newsletter can be time-consuming. If you publish one each month, you are looking at having to research, write, edit, lay out, print, and distribute or email it every four weeks, and then start all over again. Some people choose to hire a professional writer to produce their newsletters. There are also newsletter companies that will do it, providing you a packaged format and pre-written content to match your industry. You can also engage in relationship marketing by joint venturing a newsletter with another (noncompetitive) service provider or retailer, which will reduce your share of the cost.

There are many questions you must answer before you can successfully produce a newsletter:

- Who is my audience?
- What do they want to know?
- What is the purpose of my newsletter?
- What kind of information do I want it to include?
- What kind of paper and how many colors do I want (and can afford)?
- How often do I want to send it out?
- How will I distribute it? (As we mentioned in Chapter 8, if you are sending your newsletter via email, make sure you give the recipients an option to opt in or out, so that your emails will not be labeled as spam.)

A newsletter can be an excellent complement to referral marketing because it provides you with a vehicle for promoting others. By publishing brief stories about your referral resources or their businesses, you can build considerable goodwill and deliver helpful information to your readers at the same time.

4. Teach a Class

Continuing or adult education classes offered by colleges and universities, (whether in person, via tele-bridge, or online) are excellent for self-promotion and can build a reputation for you as an expert in your field. One of the great advantages of this approach to marketing yourself is that you get your name promoted in the community, you get attention and credibility for free, and you may get paid for your efforts, too.

In addition to the participants who wind up in your class, thousands of other people will become aware of you and your business when the college mails out its catalog. In effect, you get free direct mail marketing exposure to the college's entire database.

Teaching a class has other advantages:

- You can sell your product or service (NOTE: only when appropriate, and with permission).
- You can build your confidence while speaking in front of an audience.
- You can promote yourself as a public speaker.
- You can make valuable networking contacts within the academic circles of the institution where you teach.

Check your local telephone listings to identify schools in your area that might provide adult classes. Then contact the department that handles continuing education and ask them to send you information on their program and the requirements for adding your class to their curriculum.

5. Give a Speech

There are many organizations in your community that meet on a regular basis and invite speakers to address their members. Service organizations such as Rotary, Kiwanis, Optimist, and Lions Clubs meet on a weekly basis and feature speakers on a variety of subjects. Professional associations, alumni groups, and fraternal organizations may also use speakers during their meetings.

Visit your local Chamber of Commerce or your city's website to get a listing of organizations in your area. Then contact the president or the person who handles the speaker schedule or programming. Offer to send a bio and a sample of speech topics that you can address.

While there is usually no payment (other than the occasional free meal) for these speaking opportunities, they represent an excellent avenue for building your business image and making contact with movers and shakers in the business community. Take plenty of business cards and have a handout of some kind that has your name, address, and phone number on it. Do remember to avoid *selling* to your audience during your speech! Position yourself as the expert and let the confidence build into potential sales.

If you feel that you lack the public speaking skills to address these groups, you may want to consider joining Toastmasters International, an organization with chapters all over the country, which will give you the opportunity to learn basic public speaking skills in a fun, social environment. You can also check out continuing education programs offered by local colleges and universities for courses in public speaking.

6. Get Testimonials

A testimonial is a written endorsement from someone who has purchased or experienced your product or service. There are few marketing techniques that make a greater impact on potential customers than sharing the words of past customers who rave about your business.

Make it a practice to ask satisfied customers to write you a letter, in which they express their feelings and opinions about your product or service. You'll find that satisfied customers are generally more than happy to accommodate you. Be sure to tell them that you may use their comments in your promotional materials. Finally, ask them if they would please send their testimonials on their business letterhead.

7. Send Press Releases

The press release is the cornerstone of a public relations strategy. Every day, newspaper editors receive stacks of press releases from publicists, corporate PR departments, non-profit organizations, and individuals. Of course, only a small number are ever used, yet a surprisingly large number of the news stories you read every day began as a press release.

In order to have your press release read, we highly recommend you get referred to the person (editor, publisher, director of content, etc.) you want to read it, particularly in larger markets, where your press release could get lost if someone isn't looking for it. When sending by email, attach a jpeg of your logo. If you have pictures to support the news release, don't forget to include a caption to explain each one.

8. Provide Tips, Trends and Surveys

Tips, trends, and surveys are often called the "three musketeers" of marketing. Editors love them because they are brief, informative, easy to understand, and interesting.

Tips are educational tidbits of practical information presented in a concise fashion. Choose some aspect of your product or service and construct a list of five to ten things that people should know. For example, if you're an accountant, create a list of "Five Common Tax Mistakes and How to Avoid Them." If you're a real estate agent, write out the answers to, "Questions Every Home Buyer Should Ask Before Saying 'Yes.'"

Trends are current signs of where the future will be. Trends reflect the mindset and attitudes of people who are on the cutting edge of change. They tell you what's hot and what's not. If you have spotted an emerging trend related to your business, the media is probably very interested in hearing about it. Think about your current customers. What similarities do you notice about their backgrounds and buying habits? Think about recent changes in your industry. Is this something that is likely to continue and affect the way business is done in the future? If so, it may be a trend.

A survey is a more scientific approach to reporting public sentiments. It measures a quantitative response to specific questions you have posed. Surveys can be deadly dull or highly interesting: it all depends on what you ask. Make it something you and your contacts would find enlightening or entertaining. Your survey sample size should be significant enough to be worthy of reporting. The more responses you get, the more legitimate your results will be. Try to relate your survey to your field of business so that there will be a logical connection between the results and your product or service.

We suggest that you read and study *USA Today* every day for a week. This national newspaper is filled with tips, trends, and surveys. Also, watch "CNN Headline News." Between news segments, the news channel presents surveys under the heading *Fact Check*. Glance through other periodicals at your local library and look for boxes and sidebars that report this kind of information. Once you have compiled your tips, trends, or survey, report it to the media in the form of a news release. You can also share this information on your blog if you have one, or on your other social networks (see below).

9. Monitor Your Social Networking Presence

If someone posts a picture of you that shows you in a light you may not like, your image can certainly take a hit. You will want to regularly do an Internet search on yourself and your company to ensure your image is being maintained.

10. Become a Reporter's "Expert Source"

There's nothing like being quoted as an expert in the newspaper to build your credibility in the community. The trick to becoming a recognized source of information on a subject is to let the media know you exist, and to consistently educate reporters about your background and expertise.

⇒ *Action Items*

1. Create powerful vision and mission statements.
2. Evaluate the following areas of your company:

   o Logo
   o Telephone strategy
   o Facility
   o Email address
   o Collateral material
   o Website
   o You and your staff's appearance
   o Vehicles
   o Social networks

3. Take the steps necessary to correct the areas above that do not support and project your vision/mission statements.
4. Identify the PR opportunities for your company and make a press release submission calendar.

11

Your Information Network

Don't Neglect These Great Sources of Expertise and Experience

As a business professional, you need a constant supply of information to achieve success. You must stay aware of trends and issues and keep up with rapid economic and technological changes to become and stay competitive. The information component of your network consists of your most knowledgeable sources, and the people or resources that can provide you with the knowledge and expertise you need to run a successful operation.

You may have discovered already that it is next to impossible to keep up with all this information on your own. There is simply too much of it, and your own inclinations and time limitations steer you toward some kinds of knowledge and cause you to neglect others. For example, you may be strong in marketing and business planning, but weak in human resources and legal matters.

Fortunately, the knowledge you lack is always someone else's specialty, so you can turn to others for help. This is what you are preparing to do when you set up your network's information component — a web of contacts who know and understand what you must do to achieve success in your profession or business, and who have the experience to help you achieve your goals.

Step 1: Categorize Your Information Network Members

There are usually at least a few people who can help you deal with certain issues or special problems that you may encounter in the business or profession you are in, or are interested in entering. If you know you are lacking in a specific area of knowledge, you must know in advance whom to contact and where to go to get the information you need.

What sorts of people should you include in your information network?

1. **People Similar to You**

   There are some real advantages to seeking out people who have the same interests and goals as you do, and who are trying to achieve the same thing you want to achieve. They are collecting the type of information you need, and vice versa; partnering with them can help you both get it faster by dividing the research effort.

2. **People Who Are in Your Profession**

   As a rule, your best information sources will be people who are successfully doing what you want to do (perhaps in a different location or serving a different clientele). They will be aware of current trends and issues in your field, and may have already faced some of the challenges you are now facing. Try to identify and speak with three to five individuals who fit this category. They will have current directories, manuals, and information about upcoming events related to your profession, as well as relationships with vendors you may need to hire.

3. **People Who Were in Your Profession**

   Find out why these people are no longer in the profession. What happened to their business? What are they doing now? Did they make the right decision to leave the profession? Talk with people who were successful and people who were not. Depending on the industry and the length of time the person has been away from it, this information may be valuable in helping you plan.

4. **Authors**

   People who write or produce books, articles, audiotapes, and videotapes on your profession are key subject experts. They usually have broad or deep knowledge about procedures, systems, technologies, tactics, and developments in your field. A few tips from these individuals could save you money and time.

5. **Regulators**

   People who regulate, audit, or monitor professionals in your field can certainly tell you stories about the legal, procedural, and operational pitfalls that you might run into, and probably how to survive them. You may even discover legal loopholes that can make life and business easier.

6. **Trainers**

   By this we mean trainers in your field or industry. The wonderful thing about trainers is that they specialize in imparting knowledge. They help people understand the basics: they introduce new technologies, procedures, and techniques. Try to gain access to their training materials. If necessary, sign up for training sessions.

7. **Consultants**

Professionals use advisors and consultants to help them solve problems that they find difficult to handle alone or to deal with impending change. Some consultants are generalists, others, specialists. Most are skilled in assessing problems.

8. **Members of Professional Organizations**

People who are active members of trade, business, and professional organizations are prolific sources of information. Their membership gives them access to directories, newsletters, seminars, presentations, calendars of events, and more. By networking, they stay in touch with industry issues and trends. Spending time with them will help you discover new ways to do things.

Step 2: Identify Your Information Network Members

In Step 1, you got a look at the type of people who could be part of your information network. In Step 2, you should start identifying people you know in one or more of these categories. This step can be made much easier if you use a contact management system to store your contacts, especially as you start to organize your database to be used in your referral marketing plan. If you haven't got a contact management system already, we recommend an online database called Relate2Profit. Once you have uploaded your contacts, start selecting the ones that represent your information network and identify them as such.

We'd like to offer you an opportunity to try this robust database free for 30 days. Simply go to www.relate2profit.com/WBKMS and put in the coupon code WBKMS, and you will have full access to all the features of the database at no charge for 30 days, and the chance to save 50 percent for the life of your subscription, should you wish to keep using it.

Remember, it's information you're after, and more people means more information. Once you've written down as many names as you can think of, go back and fill in the contact information for each one.

⇒ *Action Items*

1. Identify 24 people who are in, or could be in, your information network.
2. Enter them into your Relate2Profit database or any contact management system that best suits your needs.

12

Your Support Network

Sources of Help and Encouragement are Closer than You May Think

Learn to rely on the people who respect, admire, and love you: they have the purest motives for helping you. They are genuinely interested in you, mostly accept you as you are, and will usually do whatever they can to help you achieve any goal. They may not have the knowledge or information you need or the ability to bring you new clients, but if you direct their willing efforts, they can give you emotional, spiritual, physical, or financial support.

Members of your network's support component can help you at crucial times in your business. They can perform essential tasks, lend you money, encourage you, work for you, help you deal with an emergency, serve as a sounding board for your ideas, even fill in for you for a couple of hours. To make the most of this resource, learn about the talents, knowledge, and contacts these supporters have to offer.

Step 1: Categorize Your Support Network Members

The people most likely to give freely of their support fall into several different categories:

Your Mentors

Perhaps even more than family members, mentors have insight into your abilities and know how to keep you focused. They may also help you in ways you aren't aware of by providing behind-the-scenes support and sponsorship.

People You Have Taught or Mentored

If you've been instrumental in another person's success by helping him gain professional knowledge and skills, that person probably owes you a debt of gratitude. These people are usually excited to hear from you and will remind you of how much they appreciate your support. They also open doors to business opportunities by constantly spreading positive word-of-mouth about you. Do the people you've mentored a favor: offer them the opportunity to pay you back. Most would be happy to support your efforts to achieve success.

People You Have Helped

People remember people who have done something for them. Can you identify people you have donated money, time, or other gifts to? Most will go out of their way to support you.

Your Co-Workers, Colleagues, Associates, and Classmates

Friends you have made in the course of your schooling and career are often friends for life. You are part of each other's history. You know, like, and respect each other. Of course, you may be reluctant to call upon a friend for help because you don't want to admit you need it. But don't let your ego get in the way — use these sources. Many of these folks will be eager to help and will not think any less of you, nor make you feel diminished for asking.

Your Family and Close Friends

You may take your family and personal friends for granted, but they are perhaps your most reliable source of support. Don't ignore them. Keep in mind, however, that some may be more reliable than others.

Fellow Members of Non-Business Groups

People you have worked with outside of business — members of neighborhood watch groups, apartment associations, community youth programs — may be willing to support you in activities outside the group's normal scope. Members of community service organizations such as Kiwanis and Lions Clubs usually make it a point to contribute to the success of other members. Join, participate, donate generously of your time, and let others help you in your endeavors.

Your Former Managers, Supervisors, and Instructors

Your former managers, supervisors, and instructors — those you admired, at least — are often familiar with your work habits, ethics, values, character, abilities, and interests. They know what it takes to get you to perform at your highest level. Often, like surrogate parents, they feel responsible for your success. You should take advantage of this 'parental' instinct!

Your Church Leaders, Members, and Groups

When it comes to giving, few places can match the spiritual and emotional support that churches provide in abundance. If you belong to a religious organization, you are bonded to others through a shared faith. It would be a mistake not to seek the backing of your church leaders and other members. If on occasion you need them, don't hesitate to use the church's support services and groups.

Step 2: Identify Your Support Network Members

Go to your Relate2profit account (or whatever contact management system you use) and type in the names of all the people you know who fit into each category — as many names as you can. Use names more than once only if you have to. The more names, the better. If one person is unable to provide the kind of support you need at a particular moment, you'll have others to fall back on. Finally, fill in the contact information for each name.

⇒ *Action Items*

1. Identify 24 people who are in, or could be in, your support network.
2. Enter them into your Relate2Profit or other contact management system database.

13

Your Referral Network

Sources of Business Opportunities Provide the Quickest Way to Success

If you can run a business entirely on the sales you make through referrals, you'll be the envy of all business owners. Someone — customer, colleague, associate, or friend — tells someone else about you, or tells you about a prospect, and the end result is a sale. Referrals are your most profitable network component, and the only way to get them is through other people.

It's important to remember that all referrals result in closed business. The likelihood of a sale depends on the method used by the Referral Source to contact the prospect, the quality of their business relationship, and other factors. Some are more likely to encounter good prospects than others; some will be more motivated to give you referrals.

Savvy professionals who know and cultivate their most likely Referral Sources get the largest number of high-quality referrals, and the more referrals they get, the more revenue they generate in the long run.

Categorize Your Referral Network Members

Some of your best sources for referrals will, of course, be the same people you consider primary sources of support and information. Others will come from entirely new categories of people, some of which may surprise you. Your best prospective Referral Sources fall into eight categories.

1. **People in Your Contact Sphere**
   A contact sphere (a group of businesses or professions that complement, rather than compete with, your business) can be a steady source of leads. It's almost a sure thing: if you put a caterer, a florist, an entertainer, a printer, a meeting planner, and a photographer in the same room for an hour, you couldn't stop them from doing business. Each has clients who can benefit from the services of the

others. This is why a wedding often turns out to be, on the side, a business networking and referral-gathering activity.

Contact Spheres

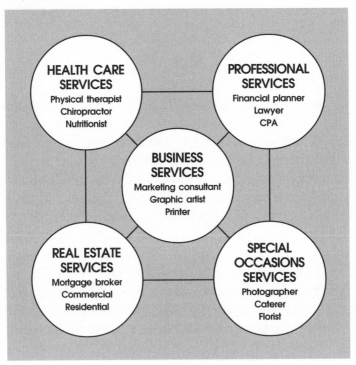

It's okay if contact spheres overlap a little — the process still works. Here are some examples of contact spheres:

- **Business services**: printers, graphic artists, specialty advertising agents, marketing consultants
- **Real estate services**: residential and commercial agents, escrow companies, title companies, mortgage brokers
- **Contractors**: painters, carpenters, plumbers, landscapers, electricians
- **Health care services**: chiropractors, physical therapists, acupuncturists, nutritionists
- **Professional services**: lawyers, CPAs, financial planners, bankers

- **Business equipment vendors**: telecom, computers, photocopiers
- **Special-occasion services**: photographers, caterers, travel agents, florists
- **Creative services:** web designers, copywriters, videographers, graphic designers

In the graphic titled Contact Spheres that appears in this chapter, you can see that each specialist in one of the contact spheres has a natural inclination to pass referrals back and forth with the others. Lawyers, CPAs, and financial planners continually refer people to one another because each works on a different aspect of the same client's financial needs. To continue with our wedding theme, a florist gets many wedding clients, and hence is in a good position to refer a photographer and a caterer; when the photographer and caterer get wedding clients of their own, they are likely to reciprocate by referring the florist. In each case, the care and feeding of contact spheres by related professions increases the opportunity to receive qualified referrals.

Notice as well that referrals can flow naturally and easily between contact spheres. The florist's wedding clients may be in need of the services of a printer (for wedding invitations), a financial planner, or a residential real estate agent. Each of these professionals may, in turn, gratefully refer other clients to the florist who sent them good business prospects.

Contact spheres can then be developed into power teams. Power teams are the people with whom you have a relationship, are in your contact sphere, and you are actively engaging in a referral relationship. We will talk about this more in Chapter 20.

2. **Satisfied Clients**

   Clients you have served well can be great Referral Sources. Having firsthand experience with your products or services, they are true believers and can communicate convincing testimonials. Keep track of these clients; they are your fans and best promoters, and they can be very effective in helping others decide to do business with you. (Keep in mind that a dissatisfied client is equally effective in turning prospects away from you!)

3. **People Whose Business Benefits from Yours**

   Of the eight kinds of people in your Referral Network, none stand to gain more than those who get more business when you get more business — business suppliers and vendors, for example. If you sell workbooks, the printer who prints them for you benefits. A related business located close to you may benefit from your customers. For example, this could be a health-food restaurant located next to your family fitness center. In these circumstances, it is obviously in the other businesses' self-interest to give you referrals.

4. **Others You Do Business with**

   Perhaps your business doesn't have anything to do with dentistry or hairstyling or automobiles, but at some point you do business with dentists, hairstylists, and auto mechanics. By contributing to the success of their business, you gain their goodwill; to keep you as a customer, they're inclined to help you secure customers of your own. If you've been using their services for some time, these vendors probably know what you do and that you're a reliable, trustworthy person. Sometimes this is all the recommendation a potential client needs.

5. **Staff Members**

   Except for customers, no one understands better than staff members how your products or services perform. We are not talking about your sales and marketing staff — generating sales is what they were hired to do. Part-time or full-time staff members in administration, production, and other functions give your business a boost when they talk with friends, neighbors, associates, and people they meet in their daily lives.

   A caveat: Keep them happy; a disgruntled employee can do your business a lot of harm. The best way we have found to keep your employees engaged in your company and its mission is to keep them informed of any changes or new directions well in advance of implementing anything new.

   Don't overlook former staff members, either. Working for your company will always be part of their history, and that history will often be part of their conversation with prospects, as well.

6. **People You've Given Referrals to**

   You're more likely to get a referral from someone you've given a referral to. The more you give, the more you'll get.

7. **People Who Have Given You Referrals**

   People who give you referrals for business or who direct others to you for networking or advice are demonstrating that they think highly of you and what you do. If they didn't, they would refer people elsewhere. Strengthen and nurture these prospective Referral Sources — don't take them for granted! Show your appreciation with personal gestures and by referring prospects to them. Call on them for further referrals, but don't abuse their generosity. Maintain the business standards that earned you their respect.

8. **Other Members of Business Referral Groups**

Referral groups are set up by their members mainly to exchange leads and referrals. A typical weekly meeting of such a group includes time devoted exclusively to networking and referring business. If you're a member, this is what you signed up for: ready access to potential new clients. To encourage communication and limit possible competitive conflicts, business referral groups often restrict membership to one person per profession or specialty.

⇒ *Action Items*

1. Identify as many professions as possible that fit within your own contact sphere.
2. Identify specific individuals who could fit into your contact sphere by going to various networking organizations, consulting your card file or database, and reconsidering the professionals you may presently be referring.
3. Identify individuals in other contact spheres with which you might exchange referrals.
4. Invite each party to participate in networking groups with you so you can formalize your relationship.

14

Making Your Network Stronger

Three Ideas for Intensifying Your Network

It has probably occurred to you that, if certain kinds of needs arose in your business, you would have no idea where to turn for information, advice, or assistance. This is not unusual. We often overlook or ignore a potential need until it becomes a pressing need. This is human nature; you're usually too busy just taking care of day-to-day business to think about emergencies that might or might not occur.

But we all know — even those of us who were never a girl scout or a boy scout — that it's best to "Be prepared." Indeed, that's largely what this book is about. Being prepared for a wide variety of situations not only serves as insurance, but also helps you establish and maintain the contacts you need to expand your referral-based business. Even if an emergency never happens, the work you do in preparing for one is not wasted: it goes into building your network.

Your network is only as strong as its weakest link. The final step in constructing it is to make it bigger, stronger, and more valuable — to intensify it. Here are three ideas that can help you do this.

Customize Your Network

Don't confine yourself to the network components and categories we've presented in the last three chapters; create others appropriate for your business or profession. For example, you might create an *industry* component with several categories of its own — engineers with whom you've collaborated, patent attorneys you know, and so on. Or you might add new categories to one or more of the existing components. Handle your new components and categories just like the others: identify at least three individuals per category.

Build Your Network

Remember, one of the key reasons you're setting up your network: to create your own *de facto* management team, a ready group of experts and contacts who can give you advice on planning and growing your business and help you handle any problems that arise. After all, if you need legal advice, would you rather know ahead of time whom to call, or just thumb through the Yellow Pages or newspaper ads? How about other areas of business — printer, secretary, interior decorator, security guard, banker, travel agent, collection agent, personnel agent? Do you know someone in each of these businesses with the experience and expertise you seek?

> One of the key reasons you're setting up your network is to create your own *de facto* management team, a ready group of experts and contacts who can give you advice on planning and growing your business and help you handle any problems that arise.

According to Harvey Mackay's *Dig Your Well Before You're Thirsty*, you should develop sources before you need them. By identifying and acquainting yourself with individuals before you need their products, services, or information, you'll save time and money and make more intelligent business decisions. And you'll know the approximate value and cost of the products and services *before* you need them.

Fill in the Voids

Now that you've identified members of your information, support, and referral network components, you should more easily be able to spot the voids and weaknesses in your network. By seeking individuals who work in these areas and filling in the voids, you will enhance the diversity, size, and strength of your network.

The End of the Beginning

By now, you should be well on your way to forming a powerful and diversified team of sources for your business or professional practice, a network that will provide you with information, support, and referrals. This systematic approach should be helping you structure your network, identify prospective members, and spotlight areas where you need to concentrate your efforts.

Several questions now arise: Have you selected the right people? Have you overlooked people you should have listed or included people you should not have? The answers depend on how well you know the individuals you have selected and how well you know your business. Perhaps you've made assumptions or failed to recall key facts about them.

Active Networking and Passive Networking

Actively networking with others means you invite those people to one or more of the networking organizations you belong to, carry several of their business cards with you all the time, and above all, refer them whenever you have an opportunity to do so. Active networking also means having a reciprocal relationship with others.

We prefer doing business with people who do business with us. Why give your business to someone who's not willing to return the favor? There are hundreds, maybe thousands, of competent, dependable business professionals in your area who provide any given product or service. They don't have to buy something from you to reciprocate. They can join one of your networking groups, carry your business cards, or simply refer you to people looking for your product or service.

Passively networking with others means that you use them as a resource occasionally but for some reason cannot actively network with them. It may be because they represent a narrow market where you have no way of assisting. Perhaps they've told you they're not interested in participating in any networking organizations. Maybe they're located too far away to refer to them regularly.

⇒ *Action Items*

1. Identify members of your information, support, and referral network components.
2. Spot the voids and weaknesses in your network, and work to improve and fill it with valuable members.

15

Making Your Company a "Hub" Firm

Connecting with Other Networks

Hub Firms

Developing effective connections with other business professionals is one of the cornerstones of building a referral-based business. A hub firm is the key business in a constellation of independent businesses tethered to one another to make the most effective use of the organizational strengths of each. Cooperative relationships between these businesses can be the source of dramatic competitive strength. Generally the firms in cooperative relationships have a contact sphere (or symbiotic) relationship. The difference here, however, is that one of the companies of this contact sphere, ideally yours, is the organizer or "hub" of the inter-related parties.

A hub firm network generally applies to consulting professions where multiple areas of expertise — or other resources that your company cannot supply directly — is required. It will allow you to operate at a higher level and provide greater service than you can alone. Some examples of businesses that would create a Hub Firm are a general contractor, wedding planner, or business consultant. A business consultant working with a client's marketing needs may need to bring in a graphic designer, a commercial photographer, and an editor. The business consultant would be the hub firm organizer and already have developed relationships with these other professionals.

In many cases this hub firm network may be unlikely to reciprocate referrals on a regular basis. Reciprocal referrals are not the primary purpose of the organizer. Being able to provide more specialized services, operating further up the food chain, and creating a competitive advantage are the motives.

Even though some of these professions may not be in your contact sphere and not able to regularly refer you, there are other ways they may be able to promote you. Some examples of ways they can support you are to feature you in their newsletter, set up a speaking engagement for you, or introduce you to people they know that are in your contact sphere.

Hub Firm

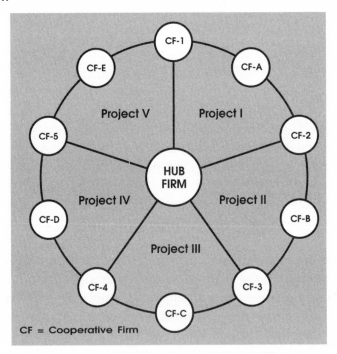

Cave Dwellers

The process of developing your company into a hub firm begins with a concerted effort to develop connections with other business professionals. According to Gene Call, a trainer and consultant from Los Angeles: "Most business people are cave dwellers. They spend their days going from cave to cave." To expand on Gene's comment: In the morning they start off in their cave at home, get into a little cave with wheels (their car), and travel to a bigger cave (their office). They stay there all day long, get back into their cave-car, and drive straight back to their cave-home. The next day they do it all over again. The irony here is that these are the people who usually say, "Gee, I wonder why I'm not getting many referrals?" Just showing up for work is not going to build your referral business. We think Will Rogers said it best: "You might be on the right track — but if you're just sitting there, you're going to get run over!"

To break out of this cave-dweller mentality and become a hub firm, you need to begin evaluating the time you're spending in your caves and take a look at some effective ways to make successful connections. The best way we've found to make invaluable long-term business contacts is through business organizations or networks.

It's important to note that one type of business organization alone cannot fulfill a comprehensive referral marketing program, no matter how small or how large your operation. A good financial planner would tell you to diversify your investments, yet we consistently see business people investing their time and money in a single business or type of organization. We recommend that you join several different types of networking groups.

Knowledge Networking vs. Referral Networking

Most people are involved in at least two types of formal networking groups. The first is intra-professional networking, or "knowledge networking," as *Megatrends* author John Naisbitt calls it. According to Naisbitt, who cited networking as one of the 10 megatrends impacting our society, knowledge networks foster self-help, information exchange, improved productivity and work life, and shared resources.

Organizations with a commonality of professional or personal interests, such as the Society for Human Resource Management and the Consumer Education Network, are good examples of knowledge networks.

The second type of networking, and the one we'll focus on primarily, is inter-professional networking: multidisciplinary professionals and occupational types who network to increase each other's business. In fact, the primary purpose of most inter-professional networking groups is to increase one another's business through referrals.

In good inter-professional networking, participants get either the majority of their business or their best business through referrals. Organizations such as the Chamber of Commerce, Jaycees, Business and Professional Women, and Business Network Int'l (BNI) are typical groups in this category.

Different groups obviously offer different strengths and weaknesses in helping you generate referral-based business. It's important to look closely at the makeup and structure of the various organizations that you might join before selecting those that best fit your needs.

If you haven't had much success in business organizations in the past, don't let that get in the way of doing what needs to be done to build your business through referrals today. This process will work if you follow it carefully. It works because it is based upon developing relationships with other successful business professionals.

The best way to begin the process is in a group or groups of other business professionals. The only alternative is to meet one person at a time, which inevitably means you're going to be working harder, not smarter.

16

Seven Kinds of Networks

How to Choose Your Contacts Strategically

Types of Networking Groups

There are at least seven types of business organizations to consider joining. Depending on your time constraints, we suggest you select at least three groups for participation. However — and this is critical — no matter what groups you end up participating in, remember something we've been teaching successful business professionals for many years:

It's not called "NET-SIT" or "NET-EAT" — it's called "NET-WORK." If you want to build a prosperous referral-based business, you must *work* the networks that you belong to!

Seven Types of Networking Business Organizations

1. Casual contact networks
2. Strong contact networks
3. Community service clubs
4. Professional associations
5. Social/business groups
6. Women's and ethnic organizations
7. Online/social networking

Seven Types of Networking Business Organizations

1. Casual Contact Networks

Casual contact networks are general business groups that allow many people from various overlapping professions. There are no restrictions on the number of people represented in any profession. These groups usually meet monthly and often hold mixers where everyone mingles informally. Casual contact networks may hold other meetings where there are presentations by guest speakers on important business topics, or to discuss issues concerning legislation, community affairs, or local business programs.

The best examples of these groups are the thousands of chambers of commerce and similar groups active across North America and elsewhere in the world. These groups offer participants an opportunity to make valuable contacts with many other business people in the community. They offer significant breadth to your goal of developing a referral-based business because they enable you to meet hundreds of other business people.

By attending chamber mixers, presentations, and other activities, you can make initial contacts that will be valuable in other aspects of developing your referral business. You can find your local chamber by calling information in your area or by contacting the U.S. Chamber of Commerce at www.uschamber.com.

A Look at the Chamber of Commerce

The United States Chamber of Commerce is one of the world's largest business federations, representing an underlying membership of businesses and organizations of all sizes, all over the country. It is organized on three levels: local, state, and national. On the national level, the national chamber helps develop local and state chambers and represents national business interests to the federal government.

State chambers coordinate local chamber programs and represent the state business community to the state government. Information on small-business programs in the state is available through the state chamber. Local chambers serve the local business community with programs in economic development (hint: mixers), community and human resources, and public affairs.

Some people have told us that they did not get much business by "networking" in their local chamber. When asked whether they attended mixers regularly, sat on any committees, attended the networking breakfasts, met with the executive director, or volunteered to be a Chamber Ambassador (a position that requires little work but provides much exposure), they always said, "No." Well, guess what — networking is a contact sport! If you want to build your business through referrals, you must be willing to get out of your 'cave' and make ongoing, effective contact with other business people. Just being a member is not enough. You must make meaningful contact with the other participants, as regularly as possible.

It's important to understand that participating in chambers or other networking group means working your way up the organization. This means taking on leadership rolls, serving on the board, or being an ambassador. Remember the VCP Process®. These roles give you an opportunity to make more contacts and move these contacts into solid relationships faster. These leadership roles also present opportunities for you to get connected with other leaders and network your way up the organization.

A Caveat

Many people try to network under the false assumption that if they belong to one chamber of commerce, belonging to three or four will bring them that much more business. You're likely to reach the point of diminishing returns quickly when you participate in several groups that are identical or even similar.

So what groups are best for you? Start by taking a hard look at the business organizations you are in or should be in. You (and your sales force, if you have one) need to be out meeting people and establishing relationships.

2. Strong Contact Networks

Strong contact networks are groups that meet weekly for the primary purpose of exchanging referrals. They often restrict membership to only one person per profession or specialty and tend to be more structured in their meeting formats than casual contact networks. Their meetings usually include:

- Open networking
- Short presentations by everyone
- A longer, more detailed presentation by one or two members
- Time devoted solely to passing business referrals

Such organizations require a far greater commitment from their membership. They usually have a set agenda, with part of the meeting dedicated to actually passing referrals you've picked up for members during

A Look at BNI (Business Network International)

BNI was created in 1985 as a way for business people to generate referrals in a structured, professional environment. The organization has grown to thousands of chapters worldwide and has generated millions of referrals for its members.

The primary purpose of BNI is to pass qualified business referrals to the members. This is accomplished by developing strong business relationships within each chapter. Each chapter follows a structured agenda that includes presentations from the members and distribution of qualified business referrals at each meeting. These referrals are tracked and recorded by the chapter officers in order to gauge the activity and success of the chapter.

the previous week. A good example of this type of organization is BNI, an organization Ivan founded in 1985 that is now one of the largest of its kind in the world.

Strong contact networks provide highly focused opportunities for you and your associates to begin developing your referral marketing campaigns. You won't meet hundreds of business people in this type of group, but all the members will be carrying your business cards around with them everywhere they go. The net result is like having up to 50 salespeople working for you! With a program like this, you will be establishing powerful long-term relationships that will prove invaluable. We highly recommend that you join one of these groups.

Don't divide your loyalties. People who join more than one strong contact network are promising their commitment to too many people. When other members discover that you've made the same commitment to people in a different group, they will eventually feel betrayed and will stop giving their business to you.

Because most strong contact networks allow only one person per profession, people who belong to two such networks and get a referral for a profession represented in both networks will have to do one of two things: give the referral to only one, which effectively reduces by half the number of referrals they hand out in either group; or worse yet, give the referral to both, with each member believing he or she is getting a good referral, which would not be the case.

We highly encourage you to select a network with a national or international base. We've seen literally hundreds of local independent groups open and close in less than a year because they lacked structure, support, and effective policies. Such groups generally turn into *coffee klatches*. They may look attractive at first because they don't have a lot of requirements and are inexpensive or free, but remember in the long run you get what you pay for.

One of the powerful benefits of being part of a larger organization with many chapters is the constant feed of new members who may hear about and join your group from members of the other chapters or groups. I have seen this in organizations such as BNI and Toastmasters. When I've spoken to these audiences, I would ask how many of them originally heard about this organization from someone other than a member of the group they participated in. I would typically get over 40 percent of the room raising their hands. This is the result of shared marketing. While one group is out marketing their group, they are creating awareness for the other groups. In the larger organizations, these referrals will pass national borders — as they did with BNI and Toastmasters. In a referral group, it only takes a few new members to bring in more business than the total of all the membership dues of all the members in the group.

— **MIKE MACEDONIO**

Several marketing books of late suggest that you assemble a local network on your own. That is an excellent suggestion, if you have lots of time on your hands and enjoy administrative tasks. Otherwise, don't reinvent the wheel. There are several groups that have been around for years that provide support and are readily available. Plug into one that's done most of the work for you already. Most important, choose one that is well supported and isn't going to fall apart next month. Stop reinventing the wheel and start looking for the wheel maker.

Strong contact networks focus on relationship building in a professional environment. If you're interested in finding out more about a networking group like this, contact BNI and ask for information on a chapter near you: www.bni.com or bni@bni.com.

3. Community Service Clubs

Community service clubs give you an opportunity to put something back into the community while doing business, making valuable contacts, and receiving good PR to boot. Community service clubs can be a fairly good source of referral-based business. Such groups exist primarily to serve the community; however, they can also provide an excellent opportunity for business people to meet regularly and develop relationships.

Although there is almost no overt networking in service club activities, you can establish long-term friendships, which are critical to the success of a solid referral-based business. Good examples of these groups include Rotary, Lions, and Kiwanis Clubs. In many ways, community service clubs were the original networks. The oldest, Rotary, was established in 1905 by Chicago lawyer Paul Harris with the idea that one person from each profession would belong and members would, among other things, help each other in business.

A Look at Rotary International

Rotary, the world's first service club, can be described in many ways. Functionally, Rotary is an association of local clubs gathered into a larger organization called "Rotary International." The individual member is a member of his local club; all clubs are members of Rotary International.

Officially, Rotary is defined as, "An organization of business and professional men and women united worldwide, who provide humanitarian service, encourage high ethical standards in all vocations, and help build good will and peace in the world."

Specifically, a Rotary Club is composed of business and professional men and women in a community who have accepted the *ideal of service* as a basis for attaining fulfillment in their personal, vocational, and community lives. Tens of thousands of Rotary Clubs Clubs meet weekly, usually for breakfast, lunch, or dinner.

Originally, Rotary was, "To promote the 'scientizing' of acquaintances as . . . an aid for success," but this early credo was dropped long ago. Although Rotary Clubs, as well as the other major service clubs, are now focused primarily on providing public service to their local communities, business is definitely conducted with fellow members. Today there are thousands of Rotary Clubs throughout most of the world, with both men and women member

(Source: Focus on Rotary, by Rotary International)

Major Community Service Organizations

Rotary International
  www.rotary.org
Optimists International
  www.optimists.org
Kiwanis
  www.kiwanis.org
Lions
  www.lionsclubs.org

You will find that your local service organizations are routinely populated with the movers and shakers of the community. If you're a member long enough, you end up befriending people who can open doors, present little-known opportunities, and help you run your business more effectively.

In 1986 I had been a member of a service club for only two months. At one luncheon meeting, the club president announced that a community center project in town was short on funds and that the fund-raising committee was seeking donations to finish construction. It seemed like a highly worthwhile project, so I got out my checkbook and began to write a check for fifty dollars. As I was writing, the president introduced two members of the club, both seated at my table, who had just donated $50,000 each! I closed my checkbook and slipped it back into my coat pocket very quietly. I didn't want anyone at the table to see that I had been writing a fifty-dollar check, when two of them had just donated a combined total of $100,000. At that very moment, I decided that these were very nice people to be having lunch with on a weekly basis.

Years later, when I had developed strong relationships with various members in this service club, I was lamenting to some of the members at my lunch table how I couldn't get a good mortgage rate on a particular property I wanted to acquire. One fellow at the table said to me, "Well, how much are you looking for?"

"One hundred fifty thousand dollars," I said.

"I've got $150,000," he replied. "When do you need it?"

"Are you kidding me?"

"No, I'm serious. I've known you a long time and I have some money that I can invest. When do you need it?"

"Next week would be okay," I said.

"Okay, fine. We can draw up an agreement next week."

"Will there be any points?"

"No, no points," he said. "Not amongst friends. Tomorrow we can work out the details."

The following week, we wrote up an agreement, and I had the money, just like that. Well, I really shouldn't say, "just like that," because I had laid the groundwork with several years of participation in this service club. As one of his committee chairmen, I had helped this individual when he was club president, and we got to know one another during this time. If that hadn't happened there would be no chance he would have trusted me enough to loan the money.

— **IVAN MISNER**

With any business organization, but particularly with service clubs, it is very important to remember that making effective contacts is a journey, not a destination. In other words, it is not something you do for a while and then stop — it is a process that you must continually follow.

4. Professional Associations

Professional associations have existed for many years. Association members tend to be from one specific type of industry, such as banking, architecture, personnel, accounting, or health. The primary purpose of a professional association is to exchange information and ideas.

Your goal in tapping into such networks is to join groups that contain your potential clients or target markets. A simple procedure for targeting key groups is to ask your best clients or customers which groups they belong to. This will give you an immediate list of at least three to five, and probably as many as ten to twelve, groups from which to choose.

Your best customers retain membership in the associations that offer the greatest value or for which there is some key strategic or competitive advantage. Similarly, the prospects you wish to target may, in many ways, operate like your best customers and have many of the same needs.

Joining such a group is like being a kid in a candy store: all that business is potentially within reach. Many groups, however, limit their membership to those who have specific industry credentials, and vendors aren't welcome (that is, if you want to join an association of accountants, you have to be an accountant).

To generate more income or to give their full members a well-rounded slate of potential vendors, a growing number of professional associations have created an *associate member* category. The associate member may not be active in the business or profession for whom the group was formed.

In associations that allow vendors as members, you're likely to encounter considerable competition. Many people have the same idea that you do. Sometimes full members are turned off because so many vendors have approached them.

If you join a group that represents your profession (and not your target market), you can still make contacts that might lead to shared opportunities with people in your profession who have a slightly different specialty or need assistance on a large project. You never know where a good referral might come from, so don't ignore this as a possible opportunity.

At the very least, a professional association of peers enables you to evaluate the marketing materials and presentations of others. By taking a good look at what works for others, you may be able to improve your own brochures, cards, or presentations.

Some examples of professional associations are these:

- American Society of Personnel Administrators
- Certified Life Underwriters Association
- National Association of Professional Organizers
- American Bar Association
- American Medical Association
- National Speakers Association

Two directories found in the reference section of any library provide the names and addresses of thousands of professional and trade associations throughout the United States: National Trade and Professional Associations and Gale's Encyclopedia of Associations. Another common reference tool is the Directory of Conventions, which provides the names, addresses, and phone numbers of specific groups that have scheduled conventions up to two years in advance. The directory is arranged geographically and even lists the numbers attending.

Locally, you can tap into the vast reservoir of the professional luncheon circuit through the business-calendar section of your local newspaper. Such calendars provide the names of groups that are meeting, the location of the meeting, the cost of the luncheon, the topic for the meeting, and either the name of the meeting planner or a number to call.

5. Social/Business Organizations

Each year, more groups spring up that serve as both business and social organizations. Groups such as the Jaycees and various singles/business clubs openly combine social activities with business or networking, giving you an opportunity to combine work with a little pleasure.

If you are interested in combining work with social activities, we recommend the Jaycees. They tend to be very focused and professional. They may be found at the following address: www.usjaycees.org

6. Women's and Ethnic Organizations

Women's and ethnic organizations have been instrumental in shaping the nature of contemporary networking organizations. With the proliferation of women business owners in the 1970s and '80s, and the difficulty they had in joining the 'old-boys' networks' in place, many women formed structured, well-organized groups that met to network and provide professional support. These groups were created not as service clubs but as bona fide networking organizations. Many made no pretenses; the members were there to network, and everything else was secondary.

A Look at NAWBO

NAWBO is a dues-based national organization representing the interests of all women entrepreneurs in all types of businesses. It is affiliated with the World Association of Women Entrepreneurs in 23 countries.

Services of the National Association of Women's Business Organizations (NAWBO) include counseling and technical assistance at the local level, primarily through networking with local members;

holding monthly programs to address problems for the female business owner; and sponsoring an annual national conference that provides management and technical assistance training through workshops and seminars.

Membership in NAWBO offers opportunities for members to expand their business horizons to national and international levels. Among the member benefits are local, national, and international networking opportunities; regional retreats, seminars, and training programs; educational programs, workshops, and seminars; international trade missions; and local, national, and international leadership and managerial opportunities. State chapters of NAWBO also offer many opportunities to make new business contacts.

These types of business organizations are very diverse in their structure and makeup. The one thing they have in common is that they tend to be concerned with education and professional development, as well as networking. Some are casual contact networks; some are strong contact networks. Others are industry-specific professional associations, such as women in construction. The benefits of membership depend on the type of group you join.

For many women, such groups can be an excellent and nonthreatening way to increase their business. Surprisingly, many women's organizations allow men in their membership. Assuming the man conducts himself professionally, he can truly benefit from membership and participation because he'll be more widely recognized as a member of a minority! You can learn more about NAWBO on its website: www.NAWBO.org

Other excellent women's and ethnic groups include the following:

- Asian Chamber of Commerce — www.asianchamber.org
- United States Hispanic Chamber of Commerce — www.ushcc.com
- National Black Chamber of Commerce - www.nationalbcc.org
- Frasernet — The #1 Network for Black Professionals Worldwide — www.frasernet.com
- American Business Women's Association - www.abwa.org
- E-Women — www.ewomennetwork.com
- Business and Professional Women/USA — www.bpwusa.org

7. Online/Social Media Networking

From a business perspective, the ideal use for social media is to build your brand and your credibility with the people you are connected to; it's about providing value for your connections and followers. It is important to offer them useful information balanced with a little personal insight and whether you're talking about face-to-face networking or online networking, credibility and relationship building is still critical to the process.

With social media, the key to success is outlining a strategy that considers the amount of time you can realistically dedicate each day to your online marketing efforts and being consistent. People have a tendency to get online at random times and start clicking away. Then something mysterious happens to the "space-time continuum" and all of a sudden two hours go by and they have nothing to show for it! Here's how to avoid falling victim to that trap — have a plan and work it! **Write up a plan for how often you will work your social media and for how long.**

Sit down and map out a weekly schedule that outlines specific days and times during which you will spend developing your social media strategy. Figure out what's realistic and what makes sense for your company and go from there. For example, if you use the micro-blogging platform called Twitter, you might schedule yourself simply to post one update at 9 a.m., one at 1 p.m, and one at 5 p.m. daily, and then dedicate ten minutes to responding to comments and messages at 10 a.m. and 3 p.m. on Mondays and Wednesdays. On Tuesdays and Thursdays, you might then dedicate ten minutes at 10 a.m. and ten minutes at 3 p.m. to "re-tweeting" people's comments that you find valuable and also thanking people for mentioning you or "re-tweeting" your posts. This is just an example, but you should definitely take the time to devise a social media strategy such as this that specifically makes sense for you.

Leverage your time! Be sure to utilize the various tools currently available that are designed specifically to save you time in your social media efforts. For example, sites like www.ping.fm, www.seesmic.com, and www.tweetdeck.com are designed to send your social media updates to multiple social networking sites, including Twitter and Facebook, with one click.

Some sites even allow you to link multiple Facebook and Twitter accounts (if you have more than one) to one desktop application where you can post updates to all sites, as well as view and respond to your friends' posts on those sites and keep a log of all your past posts. This means no more logging into multiple social networking sites — you can manage all your social networking accounts from one place!

Also, there are sites such as www.cotweet.com where you can schedule updates in advance so your updates will be posting even while you're not online. With all the traveling we do, this is a tool that we've personally found to be very useful.

Once you have your strategy in place, you will no doubt be anxious to start seeing a return on your online networking investment. It's very important to remember something we have mentioned before: Networking is more about farming than it is about hunting, whether online or face-to-face. It's about cultivating relationships with people. The bottom line is — it takes time. It is about building the credibility of your brand, and that doesn't happen overnight.

Return on Investment (ROI) is directly correlated to either — 1. Dollars spent (online paid marketing) or 2. Time and/or effort spent — in saturating and building strong profiles on whatever social media channels are deemed effective for the brand (including blogging). Don't forget that some businesses will benefit much more from spending more effort on "niche" networks that may have less traffic, but more targeted to the brand's ultimate consumer.

If your network is a mile wide and an inch deep, it will not be successful. It is important that you create a network that is both wide and deep. You do this by being visible and engaging in the conversation. Over time, this gives you credibility, which leads to building your brand and your sales and will ultimately give you the biggest ROI for your online marketing efforts.

Most of what we've discussed so far has focused on what you should do in order to carry out an effective and profitable social media campaign for your business, but there are also some things you should be sure to avoid in order to be successful.

Below are the top five common mistakes that businesses make when it comes to social media networking. Take care to avoid all of these.

Top Five Social Media Networking Mistakes

1. Spending too much time on sites you enjoy and not fully evaluating whether or not that particular site is the most effective one for your efforts.

2. Going onto a site for 'work' and then running down rabbit holes getting distracted by friends who may have posted something interesting or something that requires a response.

3. Not being able to properly define when it is more cost-effective to delegate certain social media responsibilities to someone else to handle.

4. Setting up a blog, Facebook, LinkedIn, or Twitter page and then not keeping it populated — consistency and fresh content are keys to success.

5. Forgetting that social media is about engaging in the conversation and not just about selling.

Effective networking is more about going deeper than it is about going wider.

Online networking is an outstanding enhancer to your face-to-face networking. Be careful to avoid the online networking activities that trap you in your cave!

Choosing the Networks That are the Best for You

Despite all we've covered thus far, some people tell us they simply don't have time to go to business meetings regularly. We understand that objection well. If you feel this way, let us suggest that you throw away this book, pick up your telephone, and start making cold calls instead. Or, if you prefer, open your checkbook and start writing checks for more advertising. If you're serious about developing business by referral, there is no quick fix: *you must meet people in a planned and structured way.*

Which groups should you join? Don't let chance decide where you're going to spend your time and effort. Remember, the key is to diversify your activity. Don't put all your eggs in one basket; one type of business organization won't serve all your needs. Consciously select a well-rounded mix of organizations, with no two of the same type. If you have associates, partners, or employees, consider their participation when deciding which groups each of you will target.

What If You Work for Someone Else?

We suggest that you persuade your employer that you will get business by working with these groups. Ivan can certainly attest to this from his personal experiences:

I once met a bank manager who worked hard at persuading his supervisor that participation in BNI would yield substantial results for his branch. The supervisor reluctantly agreed to let him join on a trial basis. The manager began getting referrals soon after joining.

After several months, another member gave him a particularly good referral — a man who was disgruntled with the level of service at his current bank. The manager decided to visit the man at his company. The man told the bank manager that he felt he was not getting personal service from his bank.

The manager assured him that his bank prided itself on service. He gave the man his personal pager number and home telephone number and told him that if there were a problem he could be reached any time of day, at home or at work. The man thanked him for coming to his office and told him he would get back to him.

Two days later, at 9:00 a.m., the man was standing at the bank door with several savings and checkbooks in hand. The manager met him at the door and thanked him for coming to the branch. The man said he was impressed with the way he was handled by the manager and that he had decided to transfer his accounts to the manager's bank. To the astonishment of the bank manager, the new customer handed over checking, savings, and money market accounts totaling over $950,000! After everything was completed, the man told the manager how glad he was to be referred to him by their mutual friend.

I first heard this story when my office started getting phone calls from every branch manager in Southern California who worked for that bank. Each of them wanted information about local chapters of BNI. When the bank manager who got the $950,000 referral told his supervisor where he got the referral, the supervisor (remember him? the reluctant one?) called all his other branch managers and told them to join a local chapter of their own within the next two weeks.

If you work for someone else, the lesson here is to persuade your supervisor about the benefits of networking groups! Not long ago, I spoke to an individual who wanted to join a networking group but was told by his boss that the company wouldn't pay for it. This savvy salesman asked his boss, "If I front the money myself and get two referrals that turn into sales within the next thirty days, would the company pay for it then?" The boss said, "Sure, if you come in with two sales, I'll see to it that the company pays for the membership." Well, guess what? This salesman, thus highly motivated, closed three sales and was working on four others at the end of the first thirty days. He told me that his boss "gladly paid for the original membership, and recently paid to renew it." Whether you are self-employed or work for someone else, start looking for groups that refer you new business.

— DR. IVAN MISNER

Selecting Your Networking Groups

The networking groups you choose to participate in will directly affect the success of your referral marketing effort. The following five activities will help you get your networking off to a good start.

First, determine the types of organizations that you would like or need to join. Make sure to have a good mix, for example, a casual contact network, a strong contact network, and a service club. Participate in at least three groups, but don't join more than one of each type. At the same time, be careful not to fall victim to the 'more is better' mentality. The fact that we are recommending three or more does not mean that you should participate in eight different networking groups. It is your participation in these groups, not the amount of groups that you belong to, that will make the difference. Effective networking is more about going deeper than it is about going wider. Consider your time budget when deciding to commit to networking groups.

Second, evaluate the potential networking organizations in your area that fit the profile you are looking for and select some to visit.

Third, visit as many of them as possible, and depending on the type of group.

Fourth, talk to members of each organization you visit and get testimonials on how it's been for them.

Fifth, go back and visit again before making a final decision on which group(s) to join. One time may not be enough (except for strong contact groups that may have your profession open at that moment — in that case, you may want to join before someone takes your spot. We have more on that below).

If You Snooze, You Lose

Here's some more wisdom Ivan has gleaned as founder of BNI:

If you visit a group that allows only one person per profession and you like the group, and your profession is open, don't hesitate! I kicked off a chapter of BNI (which allows only one person per profession) several years ago in Hartford, Connecticut. At the end of the meeting, two real estate agents were talking to each other at the back of the room.

I went up to them and asked if one of them planned on joining. They knew each other fairly well and one guy looked at the other and asked, "I don't know, how about you, are you going to join?"

"Well, I haven't decided," responded the associate. "I need to think about it. How about you?"

"I haven't decided, either," responded the first real estate agent. With that, he told us he had an appointment, said his goodbyes, and left.

No sooner had he crossed the threshold than his friend announced, "I've thought about it and I think I'll join!" He immediately filled out an application and joined the new chapter.

Thirty minutes after the meeting, I received a phone call from the first agent. He said, "I've been thinking about it and I decided that I should join before Charley changes his mind and decides to join."

"Gee," I said, "I don't know how to tell you this, but old Charley waited about as long as it took you to get out the door to fill out an application."

"That dog!" said the frustrated agent. "I guess I've learned that you can't blink if you want an open spot."

That experience immediately reminded me of a story I once heard about two friendly competitors who, walking through the woods one day, rounded a corner and came face to face with a huge grizzly bear. The bear was standing on its hind legs, growling and snarling. It stood over seven feet tall, looked like it weighed a thousand pounds, and was not very friendly.

One of the walkers very gently lowered his pack to the ground. Slowly, so as not to startle the bear, he opened the pack and pulled out a pair of running shoes. As he started to lace up the first shoe, his companion whispered, "You know, that bear looks as fast as he is strong."

"I know," said the man, as he finished the first shoe and began with the next.

"I've heard grizzlies can top thirty miles an hour over short distances. You can't possibly outrun him," said the other man.

"I know that, too," said the first man as he finished lacing up the other shoe.

"If you know all that," continued his friend, "why are you bothering with those sneakers?"

"Because," said the first man, as he turned his back and looked over his shoulder at his associate, "I don't have to outrun the bear — I just have to outrun you!"

The lesson behind these two stories is that if you find a strong contact group that you like and it has an opening, you'd better not blink or your competition will outrun you.

Time Investment

The secret to getting more business through networking is — to spend more time doing it! Okay, it is a little more complicated than that, because you have to spend time *doing the right things with the right people*. However, based on a recently completed Referral Institute study on business networking, we finally have a definitive answer about the amount of time people spend networking and the impact on the amount of business that is generated by that amount of time.

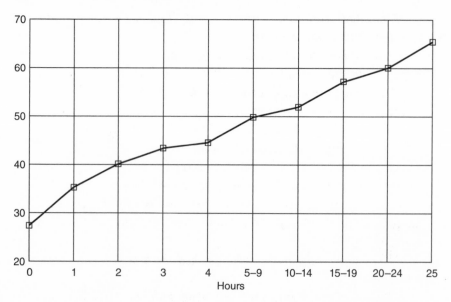

The most dramatic statistic we found in the study is that people who reported "networking played a role in their success" spent an average of 6.5 hours a week participating in networking activities. However, the majority of people who claimed "networking did NOT play a role in their success" spent 2 hours or less per week developing their network!!!

This means that there is a direct correlation between the time you devote to the process and the success that you realize from it. To illustrate this further, below you see a graph that relates to the average percentage of business generated from someone's networking efforts by the amount of time spent in networking activities. Here you can clearly see that people that are spending between 5-9 hours a week networking are generating, on average, 50 percent of all their business from this activity.

People who spend over 20 hours a week networking, on average, are getting almost 70 percent of their business through referrals!

Find the Time

This point can't be reiterated enough: Sometimes people tell us they don't have time to attend business organizations but really need to generate some more business. To this we say, "No problem. Simply increase your advertising budget by a factor of X, or hire people to start making cold calls for you, and you won't need to go to any of those darn meetings."

Find time to leave your cave and meet other qualified business professionals regularly, or you'll never develop a prosperous referral-based business. Networking is a contact sport! If you don't develop effective relationships, you can't possibly create a powerful, diverse, reliable network of contacts.

⇨ *Action Items*

Visit several types of networking groups. For each, consider these issues:

1. How long has the group been in existence?
2. What is the basic philosophy of the organization?
3. How many members does it have?
4. What is the quality of the membership?

5. How does the cost compare with other forms of marketing? How often does it meet?
6. How do other members feel about the group?
7. What is your overall impression of the group?

17

Fifteen Ways to Promote

How Your Network Can Boost Your Business

Has anyone ever said to you, "If there's anything I can do to help you with your business, let me know"? Did you respond, "Thank you — now that you mention it, there are a few things I need . . ."? Or did you say, "Well, thanks, I'll let you know"?

If you're like most of us, you aren't prepared to accept help at the moment it's offered. You let opportunity slip by because you haven't given enough thought to the kinds of help you need. You haven't made the connection between specific items or services you need and the people who can supply them. But when help is offered, it's to your advantage to be prepared and to respond by stating a specific need.

In the following chapters, you will begin to structure your network to fit your business and professional needs, and you'll identify businesses and individuals who can provide specific kinds of help that you anticipate needing when problems arise or when you need to increase your visibility, credibility, or profitability. It's a good idea, then, to have in mind the kinds of help you will want your sources to provide.

How Your Network Members Can Help You — and How *You* Can Help *Them*

Systematic referral marketing requires that you determine, as precisely as possible, the types of help you want and need. There are many ways your sources can help you promote yourself and your business and generate leads and referrals; we've chosen to discuss 15 of them. Some are simple, cheap, and quick; others are complex, costly, and time-consuming:

1. **Display Your Literature and Products**
   Your sources can exhibit your marketing materials and products in their offices or homes. If these items are displayed well, such as on a counter or a bulletin board, visitors will ask questions about them or read the information. Some may take your promotional materials and display them in other places, increasing your visibility.

2. **Distribute Information**
   Your sources can help you distribute your marketing information and materials. For example, they can include a flyer in their mailings or hand out flyers at meetings they attend. A dry cleaner attaches a coupon from the hair salon next door to each plastic bag he uses to cover his customers' clothing; a grocery store includes other businesses' marketing literature in or on its grocery bags or on the back of the printed receipt.

3. **Make an Announcement**
   When attending meetings or speaking to groups, your sources can increase your visibility by announcing an event you are involved in or a sale your business is conducting, or by setting up exhibits of your products or services. They can also invite you to make an announcement yourself.

4. **Invite You to Attend Events**
   Workshops and seminars are opportunities to increase your skills, knowledge, visibility, and contacts. Members of personal or business groups that you don't belong to can invite you to their events and programs. This gives you an opportunity to meet prospective sources and clients.

5. **Endorse Your Products and Services**
   By telling others what they've gained from using your products or services or by endorsing you in presentations or informal conversations, your network sources can encourage others to use your products or services. It would be even better if they would sing your praises on audio or video recording that you could use on your website!

6. **Nominate You for Recognition and Awards**
   Business professionals and community members often are recognized for outstanding service to their profession or community. If you've donated time or materials to a worthy cause, your sources

can nominate you for service awards. You increase your visibility both by serving and by receiving the award in a public expression of thanks. Your sources can pass the word of your recognition by word of mouth or in writing. They can even create an award, such as "Vendor of the Month," to honor your achievement.

7. **Utilize Social Networking**

   A referral partner can help you by recommending you on such platforms as Facebook, LinkedIn, Plaxo, Twitter, etc. They can use these sites to place testimonials, endorsements, a link to your site, or even an announcement about a new product or service you may have. You will want to make sure that they give a message with which you are in agreement. Also, be aware that you will need to take your professional image into consideration when making any types of photographs available for them to include in their online postings.

8. **Provide You with Referrals**

   The kind of support you'd most like to get from your sources is, of course, referrals — names and contact information for specific individuals who need your products and services. Sources can also help by giving prospects your name and number. As the number of referrals you receive increases, so does your potential for increasing the percentage of your business generated through referrals.

9. **Make Initial Contact with Prospects and Sources**

   Rather than just giving you the telephone number and address of an important prospect, a network member can phone or meet the prospect first and tell him about you. When you make contact with the prospect, he will be expecting to hear from you and will know something about you.

10. **Introduce You to Prospects**

    Your source can help you build new relationships faster by introducing you in person. She can provide you with key information about the prospect. She can also tell the prospect a few things about you, your business, how the two of you met, some of the things you and the prospect have in common, and the value of your products and services.

11. **Arrange a Meeting on Your Behalf**

    When one of your sources tells you about a person you should meet, someone you consider a key contact, he can help you immensely by coordinating a meeting. Ideally, he will not only call the contact and set a specific date, time, and location for the meeting, but he will also attend the meeting with you.

12. **Follow Up with Referrals They Have Given You**

Your sources can contact prospects they referred to you to see how things went after your first meeting, answer their questions or concerns, and reassure them that you can be trusted. They can also give you valuable feedback from the referrals about you, as well as your products or services. This is information that you might not have been able to get on your own.

13. **Publish Information for You**

Network members may be able to get information about you and your business printed in publications they subscribe to and in which they have some input or influence. For example, a source that belongs to an association that publishes a newsletter might help you get an article published or persuade the editor to run a story about you.

14. **Serve as a Sponsor**

Some of your sources may be willing to fund or sponsor a program or event you are hosting. They might let you use a meeting room, lend you equipment, authorize you to use their organization's name, or donate money or other resources.

15. **Sell Your Products and Services**

Of all the kinds of support that a source can offer, the one that has the greatest immediate impact on your bottom line is selling your product or service for you. Your network member could persuade a prospect to write a check for your product, and then have you mail or deliver the product to your new customer. If you do so swiftly and cordially, you may gain a new lifelong customer.

Marketing guru Jay Abraham has perfected the art of getting referrals from his colleagues — and a higher-powered group of colleagues would be hard to find. Vic Conant, president of Nightingale-Conant, sent a "Dear Friend" letter to his mailing list introducing Jay and telling how he had dramatically changed his business and his life. He enclosed materials describing Jay's seminars and encouraged the reader to attend one. Anthony Robbins sent a similar letter with information about Jay's book, and Denis Waitley's mail out offered Jay's audiotapes.

Suppose a customer you know well tells you a friend of his wants to buy your product. How should you respond? By telling him to have his friend contact you? By asking for information about the friend? The correct answer is neither. While the interest is still hot, let your friend, the customer, take your product and sell it to his friend, the prospect (if he plans to see his friend in the near future, of course).

Other Kinds of Help

There are other ways — with information, research, suppliers, and staffing, to name a few — your network members can help you achieve business success. Keep a list of your needs with you at all times. Add to your list as other needs occur to you. Knowing how to match your needs with the right sources is key to obtaining the types of help you need, as you saw in Chapter 11.

With a clear understanding of what you need and a handy reference in your briefcase or pocket, you'll be amazed how much easier it is to spot opportunities and find sources of support. You'll be better prepared to respond when someone says, "Let me know if there's anything I can do for you."

But remember — it's a two-way street. The 15 support activities listed in this chapter are also things you can do to help your sources promote their businesses and generate referrals. So it's a good idea to keep a list of your network members' needs with you, as well. Helping your sources achieve their goals goes a long way toward building effective and rewarding relationships.

The 15 support activities listed in this chapter are also things you can do to help your sources promote their businesses and generate referrals.

⇒ *Action Items*

1. Select three of the 15 ways to promote that you feel most comfortable and offer to do them for your best referral relationships.
2. Ask if your referral relationships would be willing to do the same for you. If they say yes, help them help you.

18

Getting to Know Your Network Members

The GAINS Approach to Getting Acquainted

In *Swim with the Sharks Without Being Eaten Alive,* Harvey Mackay says that for success in generating sales, you must know your customer: "Armed with the right knowledge, we can outsell, out manage, out motivate, and out negotiate our competitors." We believe that for success in generating referrals, it's just as crucial to know your sources, the members of your network.

By now, you should have made a list of at least some of the people you would like to include in your network. Before you recruit them, though, you need to determine how appropriate your choices are. Are your information and assumptions about each prospective member's background and expertise correct? What's your relationship with each? How well are you acquainted? Do you know them well enough to trust them? Is your relationship with each of them profitable for either of you?

In this chapter we will present five things that you and the members of your network should know about each other. We will also tell you how to get this information and use it to strengthen both new and established relationships by increasing your:

- resourcefulness
- access to valuable resources
- ability to influence and inspire others
- effectiveness in utilizing resources
- ability to identify business opportunities for you and others you know
- sphere of influence
- visibility, credibility, and profitability

The Five Elements of the GAINS Exchange

In our view, there are five things you should get to know about anyone you wish to establish a relationship with — not just business contacts, but employers, employees, association leaders and members, and potential life partners. These five things are not mysterious secrets: they are facts we are exposed to every day but often pay little attention to because we are not aware of the benefits we can accrue by sharing them. We call this sharing the GAINS Exchange:

- **G**oals
- **A**ccomplishments
- **I**nterests
- **N**etworks
- **S**kills

If you know the GAINS categories and use them effectively, you can strengthen your relationships, create stronger organizations, and live a more rewarding, productive, and enjoyable life. This is also a two-way street: Not only should you know these things about others, you should share with them the same information about yourself.

Goals

Goals are the financial, business, educational, and personal objectives you want or need to meet for yourself and for people who are important to you. They could be problems you want to resolve or decisions you need to make, either immediately or down the road; for example:

- lose 20 pounds
- relocate to Chicago
- find another job within the next six months
- raise $1,000 for the homeless
- follow up with 25 prospects per month
- write a 200-page book by the end of the year

Whatever they are, you need to define your own goals clearly and specifically, and you need to have a clear picture of the other person's goals. Indeed, the best way to develop a relationship is by helping people achieve something that's important to them. If you do, they will remember you when you need help achieving your goals. You'll become valuable sources for each of these people, and your relationships with them will endure.

You may have friends and associates who have information and resources that could help you achieve your goals, but to reap the benefits of these relationships, you have to share your goals with them. Know what you want and need. We invite you to refer to the GAINS Profile tool located at the end of this chapter. Return to it when listing your accomplishments, interests, networks, and skills, as outlined in the rest of this chapter.

Accomplishments

Some of your best insight into others comes from knowing what goals they have achieved, what projects they've completed, what they have accomplished both for themselves and for others. Accomplishments, whether as student, employee, organization member, parent, friend, sports fan, or neighbor, tell you more about a person than any number of intentions or attitudes. Your knowledge, skills, experiences, character, values, and beliefs can be surmised from your achievements. Recruiters assess job seekers' employment potential based on their accomplishments.

Your accomplishments don't have to be worthy of making the newspapers. Simple accomplishments that can tell a lot about the goals you set and how you achieve them could include:

- writing a magazine article
- building a brick wall
- reading *War and Peace*
- preparing a French dinner
- raising four kids
- walking five miles
- creating a marketing plan

People like to talk about the things they're proud of. Engage potential network members in casual conversation. Encourage them to talk about their accomplishments. You will gain insight into how appropriate they will be as network members.

Be ready to share your accomplishments with people you know and people you meet. You will naturally downplay some of them because of modesty or because you consider them insignificant or don't think you

GAINS Profile™

Use this form to record goals, accomplishments, interests, net-works, and skills—your own, or those of your Network members or others with whom you want to build a relationship. Use one form per individual; attach sheets as necessary. Date each entry so you will know how old the information is. Use the other side of this form to record information that doesn't fit one of the categories listed.

Name _Ulysses S. Grant_____ Date _4/4/62_____

Goals _Settle disagreement with Gen. Johnston's army in_

southern Tennessee; recruit Jeb Stuart to Union cause; run for

president (wait until end of war)

Accomplishments _Managed hardware business; overran Fort_
Henry; invaded Kentucky

Interests _Cigars, bourbon, military history_

Networks _Association of Yankee Generals; Distilled Spirits of_
the Month Club

Skills _Supervising large groups of unskilled workers; creating_
and resolving conflicts; managing "just in time" logistics and
inventories

did as good a job as you should have. Remember, however, that others may think more highly of these accomplishments than you do.

As you develop your list of accomplishments on the GAINS Profile tool, include not only the ones you are particularly proud of, but also any others that may do you credit.

Interests

Your interests — the things you enjoy doing, talking about, listening to, or collecting — can help you connect with others. People are more willing to spend time with those who share their interests or know something about them. Interests may include such pastimes as:

- playing sports
- reading books
- collecting coffee mugs
- watching *Jeopardy*
- listening to country music
- traveling to foreign countries

Knowing other people's interests makes it easier to find gifts they will appreciate, including information of value to them. Let them know your interests as well. If you and your network source share many of the same interests, it will strengthen your relationship.

Passions are your most important interests. A passion is something you love to do, something you could do all day long without encouragement or compliments from others. You can even be passionate about something without being good at it, but with passion, it's unlikely that you will fail to improve.

What are your interests? What are your passions? What do you love to do? Use the GAINS Profile tool to list your interests.

Networks

A network starts with any group (formal or informal), organization, institution, company, or individual you associate with for either business or personal reasons. If you graduated from Stanford University, then one of your networks is Stanford. If you work for Wal-Mart and take your daughter to Girl Scout meetings, your networks include Wal-Mart and the Girl

Scouts. If you survived the 1994 Northridge, California, earthquake, you are a *de facto* member of the Survivors of the Northridge Earthquake network.

As the saying goes, "It's not what you know, but who you know" — and to that you can add, "and those people that the people in your network know." Each of us has sources in abundance that we never use. Each member of your network is part of several other networks. Each of your prospective sources is connected, directly and indirectly, with hundreds, even thousands, of people you don't know. If you can tap the resources represented by these unknown network members, you can —

- significantly increase the potential for expanding your network and your return from networking
- assess the potential use and value of the help your networking members can provide
- select your most profitable sources more effectively
- direct and use your sources more productively
- become a better Referral Source for your own prospective sources

Skills

The more you know about the talents, abilities, and assets of the people in your network, the better equipped you are to find competent, affordable service when you or someone you know needs help. And when you're trying to round up business opportunities or simply to become more visible, your chances are much better when others know about your skills in (for example):

- negotiating
- interviewing
- budgeting
- fund-raising
- selling
- driving
- hiking

Our experience in working with prospective business owners, entrepreneurs, business professionals, and job seekers has shown that a lot of people are unaware of all the skills they possess. If you're like most, you simply perform a service or do a job without giving much thought to the skills and knowledge you use. To help you inventory your skills reliably and completely, use the Skills Inventory included in this chapter, then list your skills on the GAINS Profile tool.

Discovering Others' GAINS

There are several ways to gather information about the GAINS of your prospective network members or anyone else you may deal with. All of them are simple. None require special skills.

Listen

The easiest way to find out about a prospective network member is simply to engage him in ordinary conversation. If you listen carefully, you may learn about a problem he's trying to solve (a **Goal**), the project he just completed (an **Accomplishment**), the basketball game he watched yesterday (an **Interest**), his attorney sister (a member of one of his **Networks**), and the software he used to design an overhead (a **Skill**).

Skills Inventory

The following are some of the skills you might need to perform in many different professions. Which of these skills have you used in your career? Which are your strongest skills, the ones you are most successful at and prefer to use? List these first on your Gains Profile. Then list any others that you have.

- administering organizations
- allocating funds
- analyzing information
- analyzing organizational needs
- analyzing problems
- appraising values
- arranging social events

- assembling equipment
- auditing accounts
- auditing operations
- brainstorming
- calculating numerical data
- checking accuracy
- coaching
- communicating
- compiling data

- conducting meetings
- coordinating computer networks
- coordinating tasks
- corresponding in writing
- counseling
- creating work environments

- delegating responsibility
- designing information systems
- developing projects
- directing programs
- disseminating information
- distributing products
- editing
- entertaining
- establishing standards
- evaluating results
- evaluating services
- maintaining equipment
- maintaining records

- making recommendations
- managing organizations
- marketing products or services
- mediating
- monitoring progress
- motivating employees
- negotiating contracts
- operating equipment
- organizing tasks
- persuading
- planning activities
- preparing publicity
- preparing reports

- presenting ideas
- programming computers
- promoting events
- protecting property
- raising funds
- recording information
- recruiting
- repairing equipment
- researching
- scheduling
- selling
- setting agendas
- setting policy
- solving problems
- troubleshooting
- others not listed here

It's not always that easy, of course, but once you discover an individual's interests or, even better, his passions, you tap into information that will help you build a much stronger relationship, particularly if you share that interest or passion.

Observe

Want to know more about your prospective network member? Be a detective. Watch where he goes and with whom he spends his time:

- What kind of car does he drive?
- What does his bumper sticker say?
- What books does he read?
- What colors does he wear?
- When you see him away from the office, is he carrying a tennis racket, a toddler, a backpack, a sack of fertilizer?
- Does he wear a T-shirt that says BUNGEE BANZAI?

You'll be surprised at how much you can learn by just watching and thinking about what you see.

Ask Questions

Do you have a good, open, friendly relationship with your prospective network member? If you do, your best way of finding out her GAINS may simply be to ask her. If that seems too direct, however, you can learn a lot by asking indirect, conversational questions. What exciting things did she do this weekend? What good movies has she seen lately? How has her year gone? This is the way most of us get to know our friends and acquaintances.

Review Written Materials

Another way to discover your network prospect's GAINS is to review all of his promotional materials — brochures, business cards, newsletters, press releases, notes — that you can get your hands on. If he's made a record of his knowledge or skills, such as a book or an instructional audiotape or videotape, get a copy and pay close attention.

Ask Others

Anyone who has contact with a prospective network member or other person you deal with is a source of information. Without coming across as an investigator, ask her a few questions about her relationship with your target. For example,

- How long has she known X?
- How well does she know X?
- What opportunity has she had to work with X?

Share Your GAINS

People are more likely to share information with you if you share information with them. Take the initiative: share a goal, accomplishment, or interest with a prospective network member. He will probably respond in a kindly manner. You can get the ball rolling by describing some of your priorities. Then, looking for an opportunity to offer help, ask, "What are some of your priorities for this week or month?"

Recording the GAINS You Discover

As you discover the GAINS of the people you are interested in, keep a record; otherwise, you're likely to forget important information. Use the GAINS Profile tool we've included in this chapter. Relate2Profit, the database service we have mentioned in previous chapters, is specially designed to record the facts you learn about your most important contacts. When you don't have a GAINS Profile with you, keep detailed notes on whatever you have (you could even call your home phone and leave yourself a message). Label each item G, A, I, N, or S for easy reference. Later, add the new information to that person's GAINS Profile, or simply drop the note into his file.

Here's a story from Ivan that truly illustrates the value of a GAINS exchange:

> I once had the chance to see how this literally transformed a networking relationship between two businessmen who had been in the same networking group for quite some time, but had not really made that deeper connection with each other.
>
> They begrudgingly took my recommendation to do the GAINS exchange and found that they had quite a few similar interests, achievements, and successes! They both coached their young son's soccer teams; they both had a hobby of collecting sports teams' hats; and they both had received their college degrees in the same field.
>
> You never saw two such seemingly disinterested people become very close and develop the closest type of networking relationship, one that most only dream about having with their referral partners. This was possible only because of doing the GAINS exchange! In fact, the GAINS exchange led to a friendship that resulted in an exponential increase in referrals between them.

We hope that by now you can see what we mean about networking being as much a mindset as it is a skill set. Clearly there are many things to *do* that will make your networking attempts successful, but there are also a good many things to *be* that are equally, if not more, important to this art.

GAINS Too Easy?

If you think that getting to know the GAINS of the people you deal with is too easy and you need a greater challenge, we have two recommendations:

- First, see if you can identify the GAINS profile for *each* member of your network.
- If you feel the need for an even greater challenge, get a copy of Harvey Mackay's *Swim with the Sharks Without Being Eaten Alive* and test your knowledge of the most important people in your network using his 66-question customer profile.

One of the most remarkable things about Harvey Mackay, author of *Swim with the Sharks Without Being Eaten Alive*, is his constant recollection of previous conversations. Over the years, I have had numerous conversations with Harvey Mackay. What continues to impress me is how he always recalls virtually everything we have ever spoken about, and it doesn't matter if the conversation was a couple of days ago or months ago. Having read Harvey's book, I know that he doesn't have a photographic memory. What I do know is he has a system to record key points so he can recall them on future meetings. For me, that works, and I'm impressed.

— IVAN MISNER

Quality Time

How well do you know the people you want to include in your network? Chances are you have a little homework to do. You can't know everything about them, though; that's why we recommend that you focus on the five keys in the GAINS exchange.

Spend more time with the people you already know, particularly with those you believe you know well. Concentrate on learning these five essentials — their goals, accomplishments, interests, networks, and skills. Be prepared to discover new things. Find overlapping areas of knowledge and interest. Make sure you give back the same kinds of information. The more they know about you, the faster your name will come to mind when an opportunity arises in which your products, services, knowledge, skills, or experience might play a part.

Matching Needs with Sources

Now that you've identified the kinds of support you need and gotten better acquainted with your network members, you're ready to make a preliminary decision about which of your prospective sources can provide you with the help you want.

Matching Needs and Prospective Sources

Help Needed	Sources to Contact
Publicity	Al Sharpton
Insurance	Lloyd Wausau
Transportation	Craig Breedlove

Based on what you know about your network members, determine the type of help you prefer from each. At this point, consider primarily each network member's qualifications to provide the specific kind of product or service you need. Other factors that will influence how you match needs and sources include the network member's availability, flexibility, and interests. You may have sources that are capable, but if they're not interested in helping you or don't have time to help you, it's not a good match.

You may not yet have enough information to identify a source for every need, but now you know where to focus your research. The more you know about your prospective sources, the easier the matching process will be. You will inevitably discover that some of your sources do not have the talent you thought they had, and others will have capabilities you weren't aware of before.

⇛ *Action Items*

1. Complete a GAINS profile for yourself.
2. Find out the GAINS profile of your top five referral relationships.
3. Share your profile with each of them.

GAINS PROFILE™ (Page 1/3)

Your partner's name	Date

PERSONAL INFORMATION

Nickname

Date and place of birth

Favorite color or food

Best friend

Mentor/sponsor/role model/hero

Favorite TV program/song/hobby

A personal award or recognition

Type of pet or vehicle

GOALS

ACCOMPLISHMENTS

INTERESTS

NETWORKS

SKILLS

19

Eighteen Ways to Motivate Your Sources

Inspiring Your Network Members to Help You

Now that you've identified your strategic sources — the members of your network — how do you go about generating information, support, and referrals from them? Some people use what might be called the 'hope' strategy: They provide great products and service, and then sit back and hope that referrals will come their way.

The good news is that such passive strategies do actually work. When they are pleased with your products or services, your customers tell others, and should someone ask for a recommendation, your name is likely to be mentioned.

The better news is that you can improve your access to information, support, and referrals by using a more active strategy. You may find this encouraging; if you're like most entrepreneurs, you'd rather do something to get things moving than sit around waiting for things to happen.

In this chapter, we describe 18 tactics you can use to motivate your network members. Some of these are direct; that is, you specifically ask for business support or referrals. Others are indirect; they stimulate referrals and support as a result of your taking certain actions. The first 14 apply primarily to relationship building, while the last four directly to referral generation. We will focus our discussion on four aspects of each tactic:

1. **Its purpose or goal**

   Contacting a source to ask for help can be embarrassing, especially if you haven't been in touch. It's also likely to fail to get results, because your source may feel he is being used. You should make it a point to contact your network members regularly for other reasons — to offer something of value, such as your help or a business opportunity. By doing so, you gain visibility, respect, and gratitude. When you use one of these tactics to provide a network source something of value, there's usually an explicit or implicit understanding that you will receive something in return. Your choice of tactics has a major impact on how successful this arrangement will be.

2. **Its benefits**
   When you contact a source and employ one of these 18 tactics, you expect to derive certain benefits. Make sure the outcome you expect matches your overall mission.

3. **Its key action steps**
   Making a tactic work requires planning and following a series of steps. The procedures we have outlined here for each tactic, however, should be considered guidelines, not hard-and-fast rules. Customize these steps to fit your particular situation.

4. **Its applicability and requirements**
   Some tactics work better with certain kinds of contacts than with others. Our discussion will help you choose the most suitable tactic for approaching each of your contacts.

Tactic 1. Volunteering

Purpose

Offering your assistance on a network member's project or assignment strengthens your cooperative bonds (see also Tactic 15, Collaborating; Tactic 16, Sponsoring; and Tactic 17, Promoting).

Benefits

Helping your network member achieve an important goal gives you authority to make contact and spend time with him. Besides your initial meeting, you will need to schedule follow-up meetings, receive guidance, get his approval on actions, and provide status reports. The more opportunities he has to observe your follow-through on your commitment, the more he will trust you.

There are two benefits to using this tactic. When your voluntary contributions don't relate to your expertise or business, you are at least establishing trust, reliability, and friendship. When your help comes from your expertise or business, you are also building your business credibility and encouraging future business dealings and referrals.

Steps

- Select your volunteer assignments strategically.
- Investigate what needs to be done before you offer help.
- Offer to spend time, either short term or over a longer period, advising your network member or helping him achieve a goal or complete a project for which he is responsible.
- Provide whatever type of assistance your network member needs, whether or not it is related to your expertise or business specialty.

Applicability and Requirements

- Set limitations up front on what you have to give and make sure your help is wanted under those conditions.
- Before you commit, make sure you know your target's level of commitment.
- Seek assignments that keep you in contact with your target.
- Look for ways you can help that are easy for you to do but that your target considers high-value support.
- Deliver on your commitments; otherwise, your source may conclude that you are not dependable.

Tactic 2. Recruiting

Purpose

A prestigious or influential role in your business, whether formal or informal, short term or long term, can mean authority and other benefits for a source. Offer a network member the opportunity to serve on your board of directors or your advisory board, to make a presentation to an important group, to write an article for a key publication, or to serve as a judge for a contest you are sponsoring.

Benefits

Many people consider it an honor to be asked to assume a key role because it enhances their image as an involved and respected leader. It also lets your sources get to know more about you and other people you know and gives you license to stay in contact with them. This approach will help familiarize your network members with your business and profession.

Steps

- Identify the roles and assignments you have to offer.
- Identify the individual you want to assume each role.
- Write or call to offer the assignment or role. Describe the role, the time required, the reason the network member was selected, the benefits the network member will receive, and a response deadline.

Applicability and Requirements

- Spell out clearly the benefits of being involved.
- Avoid creating a financial obligation for your source, and keep to a minimum the time she needs to invest.
- Let her know that she should accept only if she truly wants to. Encourage her to try it for a while, and let her know that she can quit at any time if it becomes a burden.
- It's best to develop a strong bond of trust before using this approach.

Tactic 3. Researching

Purpose

The goal of this tactic is to persuade your network members to participate in some form of research.

Benefits

This tactic helps you get to know your target market and its needs better. If done well, your research will stimulate your prospective sources' interest in one of your areas of expertise, enhance their knowledge, and generate valuable buzz about yourself and your profession. You may even generate new ideas for your business.

Steps

- Design a research project — perhaps a simple survey or a complex questionnaire — on a topic related to your field that you believe will interest your sources.
- Ask your network members whether they would be willing to participate in some research you are conducting; give them background information about the process, your goals, and how you expect to use the results.

Applicability and Requirements

- Keep your research short, simple, and interesting.
- Since the research approach is one in which you are asking for something from your sources, it is crucial that you follow up with thanks and a summary of the results.

Tactic 4. Reporting

Purpose

Playing the role of reporter is a good way of eliciting information and advice from a network member — for example, by interviewing him for an article or while doing research on a subject he is familiar with.

Benefits

The reporting approach benefits you in two ways: You learn more about your network member, and he appreciates the visibility you give him. He will probably be more willing to meet and cooperate with you in other situations, thereby strengthening your relationship. Others will seek you out as an authority or ask you to do articles or research on them. People in business like exposure, especially if it's free.

Steps

- Interview your subject to get information worthy of being publicized. It could be something he is doing or has achieved, or simply his opinion.
- Take pictures of and with your subject when appropriate.
- Publish the information for its largest possible audience, whether in school, church, community, local, trade, or national publications.

Applicability and Requirements

- If appropriate, offer to include your network member's name in any article or research he has contributed information to.
- Distribute complimentary copies of your articles or findings to people important to your targets.
- Make no guarantees that what you write will be published.

Tactic 5. Source Seeking

Purpose

This tactic involves contacting your prospective sources to identify people they know who can help you achieve a particular goal. For example, you may ask a source to name someone who:

- can help you with a problem
- can sell you something you want
- owns something you want
- knows someone in a certain area
- has been somewhere you want to go

Benefits

Using this approach will help you save time and money, increase your number of sources, discover some of your best sources and opportunities, and broaden your knowledge of your sources' networks.

Steps

- Determine what you need, and be as clear as possible.
- Identify which sources you will contact for recommendations.
- Contact more than one source for a recommendation; this way, you may find several prospects that can help you with a particular problem.
- Be sure to let your sources know approximately how many options you plan to investigate before you make a final decision.

Applicability and Requirements

- Be aware that some of your sources may be protective about the people in their network. They may want to check with their contacts before they give you their names and numbers.
- Since this approach is primarily one in which your sources give to you, it is important to follow up with thanks and status reports. Be sure to let them know your final decision.

Tactic 6. Advice Seeking

Purpose

The purpose of seeking advice is self-explanatory: You need advice, and you ask a network member for it.

Benefits

People like for others to listen to their opinions and advice. By inviting them to talk, you can get better acquainted with their knowledge, decision-making ability, and attitudes. Receiving someone's advice gives you a reason to contact her again, thank her, and let her know what you plan to do. This is a great way to keep your resources informed and, of course, to get their opinions about what you are doing.

Steps

- Ask your network member for advice or opinions on something she enjoys talking about and to which you expect her to have an answer.
- Listen carefully and respond appropriately. Direct your questions toward what your network member says in conversation; for example, "You made a comment earlier about high-growth investments. What do you think about this no-load fund I've been hearing about?"

Applicability and Requirements

- Have a logical reason for wanting the information.
- Avoid potentially controversial and sensitive issues.
- Don't ask your network member to give you advice that she would otherwise charge you for.
- People are more likely to remember their own words than others'. If you want someone to remember your conversation, let her do most of the talking.

Tactic 7. Advising

Purpose

This tactic involves giving your prospective sources valuable advice (related to your specialty or profession if possible) such as advance notice of a change in procedures, tips on how to initiate the change, or other information that can help your network member achieve satisfaction or success (see also Tactic 6, Advice Seeking, and Tactic 8, Announcing).

Benefits

One of your goals is to get network members to feel that you are a link to privileged information — that you're an insider. The advice you give may lead your prospective sources to seek you out for answers to their questions or to feel that you're looking out for their best interests. It's a great way to remind your prospective sources of what you do.

Steps

- List the topics that you feel comfortable giving advice on, and then list network members who might need advice on each topic.
- Decide whether you will apply this tactic formally, such as by newsletter, or informally, such as in a personal note.
- Decide how frequently you will send updates.
- Ask your sources to name others who might benefit from your advice.

Applicability and Requirements

- Periodically ask your network members whether they find your advice useful.
- Tell your network members to let you know if they don't wish to receive your updates.

Tactic 8. Announcing

Purpose

Providing information about upcoming events and opportunities helps make and maintain contacts. The events can be of either business or personal interest, as long as the nature of the function appeals to your audience.

Benefits

Using this approach will cause your audience to view you as an information source and to come to you with questions about other events.

Steps

- Determine what information your network members would like to have but do not currently receive.
- Identify individuals and groups that value what you have to share.
- When conducting or attending meetings, conferences, or other gatherings, make announcements about upcoming conferences,

seminars, shows, meetings, television programs, contests, application deadlines, and other events.
- You can also use this tactic by disseminating written announcements via "snail" mail, email, or other means.

Applicability and Requirements

- Don't tell people what they already know; the less likely it is that your audience could have heard the information from another source, the better.
- Announce two or three events at a time.
- Don't give away everything in the announcement; ask your audience to contact you individually for details.

Tactic 9. Shopping

Purpose

A good tactic for motivating a network member is to let her know that you are in the market for her product or service (see also Tactic 10, Purchasing).

Benefits

Your money is one of your best networking tools. Businesspeople pay a lot of attention to prospective clients and will try to sell you on their products and services. This can lead to greater cooperation and bring opportunities to share information, support, and referrals.

Steps

- Let your prospective source know that you plan to explore a few options before making your purchase.
- Find out from her customers how they are treated.
- Make your purchasing decision within a reasonable time.
- Let her know what factors influenced your decision.

Applicability and Requirements

- Once you've made a purchase, especially a large, one-time purchase such as life insurance or a house, you may find that your
  source's attention wanes. Therefore, be sure to take full advantage
  of the attention you get as her prospect.
- Don't apply this tactic to insignificant purchases; buying a tube of
  toothpaste does not call for a commitment.
- Don't play games; if you're not really interested, don't lead her on.
- Using this approach is definitely a way to test your prospective
  source's patience and attitude. Does she want to help you meet
  your needs or just make a quick sale?

Tactic 10. Purchasing

Purpose

One of the friendliest and most natural ways to make contact with a source
is to buy his products or services, whether in large or small dollar amounts.
The purchase doesn't necessarily have to be from his primary line of business — perhaps a ticket to a fund raiser, a used car, a computer, or even a
box of Girl Scout cookies from his daughter.

Benefits

By purchasing something from your network member, you become one of
his customers. As a customer, you are high on his priority list; he will be
more inclined to do business with you and give you information, support,
and referrals. This approach also increases your source's interest in getting
to know you and staying in touch.

Steps

- Analyze how you are spending your money now.
- Decide how much you want to spend.
- Test your relationship with the people you buy from now. Do they
  know you? Do you benefit from doing business with them?

- Identify the products and services your sources offer that you want or need — or the purchase of which might benefit your business in the long run.

Applicability and Requirements

- Are you buying products and services from people and organizations that see you as an individual? Do the people you buy from know your name, and think of you as their customer? There's a big difference between being a customer of Sears and being a customer of Joe's Shoe Store.
- Use your purchasing power in a way that gives you more benefits and builds relationships. Buy at least half of your products and services from people you know; however, don't do it in a way that makes them feel obligated to buy things from you.

Tactic 11. Connecting

Purpose

Connecting is a tactic designed to help a network member expand his network of business and personal friends and sources.

Benefits

Any help you can give a network member in achieving success and satisfaction strengthens your bond and enhances your image as a resourceful, well-connected individual.

Steps

- Introduce your network member to people who share his interests and who may be able to give her the information, resources, services, support, or inspiration he needs.
- Coordinate your network member's first meeting with your contact and give them both enough background information to get the relationship off to a quick and productive start.

- In your introduction, include their names, occupations, how you met, the nature of your relationship, a brief description of each person's business, and why each is a person the other should know.

Applicability and Requirements

- It's important to know what kinds of people your prospective source wants to meet; if you're not sure, ask. Likely candidates are people in your target's occupation or contact sphere.

Tactic 12. Inviting

Purpose

You can enhance your contact with a prospective source by inviting him to an event you are attending, hosting, or one in which you are participating as a featured guest, exhibitor, panel speaker, or award recipient.

Benefits

Inviting them to your events keeps your targets informed of activities you are involved in. When the event is one where you have an opportunity to share your expertise or where you are being recognized for an achievement, using this tactic contributes to building your credibility and image as a successful and knowledgeable professional. This tactic also helps acquaint your targets with others in your network and transforms strictly business relationships into friendships.

Steps

- Make a list of the events you will be attending and a list of network members you might invite.
- Allowing plenty of lead-time, call or write each prospective source to invite him or her to the event; explain the reason for the invitation.
- Pay your network member's admission fee, if there is one.

Applicability and Requirements

- Make sure the event offers benefits to your prospective sources, such as an opportunity to meet someone they admire, to be entertained, or to be recognized.
- Whenever possible, allow your guests to invite guests of their own.
- It's okay to invite people you do not expect to attend. Remember, one of your aims is to keep your sources informed of what you are doing.

Tactic 13. Recognizing

Purpose

By recognizing your sources for contributing to your business success, you help them both enhance their image and increase their visibility.

Benefits

When others ask your target source about the recognition he has received, it leads to a discussion of his relationship with you or your business and stimulates buzz about your sources. It tells other people and sources that someone trusts you, and it makes it easier for them to trust and support you.

Steps

- Publicly compliment, express appreciation, and reward your members for their support, leads, referrals, information, and business, for example, with a Customer of the Month contest whereby the winner is awarded a certificate, gets his picture posted on a bulletin board, or is written about in a local newspaper.

Applicability and Requirements

- Make sure the recognition and rewards you give are appropriate and that the recipients are worthy.

- Be sincere in your compliments. Share the recognition with the kind of people your prospective sources would like to impress.
- Don't overdo it; extravagant praise may embarrass your target and sound insincere.

Tactic 14. Horn Tooting

Purpose

The idea behind tooting your own horn is to let your sources know about achievements you are particularly proud of.

Benefits

Properly used, this approach will generate interest in you and your business or profession. It should get others to seek you out, ask you questions, and feel that you are knowledgeable and confident. Using this approach may help uncover needs, interests, and achievements that you share with your prospective sources. If you avoid looking like you're just bragging, it will help familiarize others with the services or products you sell.

Steps

- During everyday conversations, phone calls, and introductions, casually keep your sources informed about your achievements, plans, assets, and networks.
- You can also do a little low-key horn tooting through email or other correspondence.

Applicability and Requirements

- Remember, your purpose is not to brag; rather, you want to share with your sources, in a modest way, some of the things you've achieved.

Tactic 15. Collaborating

Purpose

The collaborating tactic is used to express interest in establishing an informal partnership with a contact for your mutual benefit.

Benefits

One of the best ways to obtain a commitment from a network member is to make a commitment to share resources and efforts. Collaborating creates a reliable and committed source of information, support, and referrals and helps you achieve your goals more easily and quickly.

Ivan's co-author of his best-selling *Business By Referral*, Robert Davis, produced a very successful audiocassette program, *Total Quality Introductions*, through collaboration with Laura Miller. Neither of them had a product, but they knew that developing products could significantly enhance their success as trainers and speakers. They shared costs, time, and resources; they encouraged each other; their relationship grew stronger. It took about a year, but they got the tape done much sooner than they would have by doing it alone. Since that project they have individually produced other tapes and products, but it was the initial collaboration that got them off the ground.

Steps

- Decide on what kinds of resources you need to obtain: information, support, or referrals.
- Select a prospective source.
- Meet with the source to discuss the type of partnership, your needs and resources, and her needs and resources.
- Frame an informal agreement on how the partnership will work: what resources you will share, how you will share them, and for how long.

Applicability and Requirements

- You and your partner must be very clear about what you want and expect from each other. Select someone you trust, someone who will pursue goals with as much energy as you.
- If you can, set up a trial collaboration before you establish a long-term commitment.

Tactic 16. Sponsoring

Purpose

The purpose of sponsoring is to help your sources by providing financial and resource backing for projects or programs with which they are involved.

Benefits

Sponsoring a program or event gives you an opportunity to work with sources and prospective customers for a definite period. When you sponsor an event or activity, you usually communicate with many people through correspondence, personal introductions, promotional literature, signs, and banners. By doing so, you gain exposure to potential customers or influential individuals in your target market, people who can provide business support and referrals. Other benefits, such as display and distribution of your promotional materials, can be negotiated.

Steps

- Select an organization or individual you want to sponsor.
- Decide how you wish to benefit the company.
- Negotiate the benefits.

Applicability and Requirements

- It's important to select a project or program that suits your beliefs, values, philosophy, and goals.

- Use this approach with sources that have a strong relationship with individuals and organizations in one of your target markets.

Tactic 17. Promoting

Purpose

This tactic is designed to get information, support, and referrals by providing promotional support to your sources; to demonstrate to them how well you know them and trust them; and to help build relationships between them and other members of your network. **TAKE NOTE:** Because this is an indirect approach, there's no guarantee that you'll receive promotional support and referrals in return.

Benefits

Helping your sources get business makes them more likely to help you get business. By letting them know exactly what actions you have taken on their behalf, you give them a model for generating business for you.

Steps

- Introduce a member of your network to another member or acquaintance. Describe your network member's background and business and how well she performs.
- Let the other person know that if he ever needs the kind of products or services offered by your network member, he should not hesitate to call on her.
- Promote your network member as often as possible, whether or not she is present — for example, by nominating her for an award or using her as an example in presentations and introductions.

Applicability and Requirements

- Be selective with this approach, and truthful about your network members; you don't think the world of everyone.
- Don't make your sources feel obligated because you have promoted them or generated business for them.

- Be patient, continue to give strategically, and the business support and referrals you want will come.

Tactic 18. Auditing

Purpose

Auditing is a two-tiered tactic. Initially, its purpose is to obtain feedback and suggestions from clients and observers on their experience with your products and services. If the information you receive is positive, contact your sources again to solicit their involvement in some of your promotional activities or to request permission to use their feedback in your promotional campaign.

Benefits

Using this approach will help you identify your true believers and champions. You'll generate ideas on how to make things better and you'll capture clients' opinions in writing. This approach will help you discover new opportunities and spot problems early. Most important, it will help you generate testimonial statements, endorsements, and referrals.

Steps

- Design an oral or written survey or questionnaire.
- Identify the group you will survey.
- Get feedback from your sources on the quality of your products and services by conducting surveys during or immediately after delivery of your service or product.

Applicability and Requirements

- Use this approach with sources that have firsthand knowledge of your products or services, and get their feedback as close to the delivery point as possible.
- Be sure to let your sources know how you used their feedback.

Choosing the Best Tactics

You now have the outlines of 18 tactics that you can use to cause your network members to want to provide you with information, support, and referrals. Your decision on which to use, and with which sources, depends on the situation, your personal and professional style, and the results you expect to achieve.

⇒ *Action Items*

1. Select three tactics that you feel can be implemented this week with members of your network.
2. Track any responses that you see by using the tactics.
3. Do the same thing with three different tactics next week.

20

Recruiting Referral Sources

Getting Your Network Members on Board

Let's assume you've applied one or more of the techniques described in the last chapter and have received a referral — better yet, lots of referrals. What do you do next? Just sit back and watch the money roll in? No way! You've still got lots of work to do!

Getting referrals is great — however, until your prospect makes a purchase, you're looking at only *potential* business. The number of referrals you convert into customers measures the true success of your efforts. That's what this chapter and the four that follow will show you how to do: generate referrals and turn them into customers and business opportunities.

Our method of generating and using referrals has five phases:

1. recruiting the prospective Referral Source
2. briefing the Referral Source
3. priming the prospect (source's action)
4. initiating contact with the prospect
5. rewarding your Referral Source

These are the five phases involved in activating your referral network. Familiarize yourself with all five phases before you begin — you'll find it a lot easier to understand and apply the method. This chapter describes the first of these phases: recruiting the Referral Source.

Active, Not Passive

The only way to generate referrals is through other people. Although this five-phase method can work with new and developing relationships, we have designed it to be used primarily with strong relationships, people with whom you share a strong common interest over a long period.

The heart of the method is active, not passive, recruitment. You can, of course, put the system in motion the moment someone tells you she knows someone who may need your products or services. But don't wait around for referrals — go find them. The more high-quality referrals you can generate, the better your business will be.

You should recruit Referral Sources that meet the follow six criteria:

1. those who want to, or can be inspired to, help you
2. Those who have time, or are willing to make the time, to help you
3. Those who have the ability, or can be trained to do, the things you want them to do
4. Those who have the resources necessary to help you
5. Those who have relationships with the types of people you want to target
6. Those who would make good referrals for people you know

It is crucial that your sources meet all six criteria, in order to guarantee a long-term, sustainable referral relationship. Time and time again we have worked with frustrated business owners who can't understand why they are not getting the referrals they should. On the surface, they seem to be doing all the right things. In many cases they discover that they have misdiagnosed the VCP Process® with their Referral Sources, or they are actively working with Referral Sources that don't meet all six of the above criteria.

If you've understood this book thus far, and if you've completed the assignments and action items, you've already done most of the work necessary for turning referrals into business. You've selected prospective Referral Sources. To strengthen your relationships with them, you've learned more about their GAINS and better acquainted them with yours. You've thought about the specific kinds of help you'll need from them. And although a strong relationship with them is by itself one of the best referral generators, you've decided to use other tactics as well. One of the best ways to motivate your sources is to offer them help in using this referral-generating system to get their own customers and business opportunities.

Initial Contact

After you've compiled your list of excellent prospective Referral Sources, your next action is to begin contacting them. What's the best way to get your message to them? Should you send them a letter, email or fax them, or arrange to meet them in person? Any of these formats could work; however, your first communication with a prospective source is best done by telephone. It's more personal and friendly than a written message, but it is more convenient for both you and your source than a face-to-face meeting.

Before you call, plan your call carefully. Decide which topics you want to cover. Remember, the purpose of your call is to ask for support in generating referrals, to give a brief overview of your plans, and to schedule an appointment to discuss your plans in detail. Here are a few guidelines:

- Begin with an appropriate greeting and small talk.
- State the purpose of your call and the amount of time you need.
- Ask whether this is a good time to talk.
- Get into the heart of your conversation by offering the person you are calling something of value. For example, explain how the topics you want to cover will help him.
- Tell your prospective source that you'd like to have his help in generating referrals for your business and ask for a meeting to discuss the details.
- Schedule a face-to-face meeting or a telephone conference.
- Tell him you have some information for him to review (this will be covered in the next chapter).

Scripting Your Call

Although you shouldn't expect to follow it mechanically, you may find it useful to prepare a script to anticipate how your first contact may go. To show you how to do this, we'll invent a fictional character, Dr. Mark Star, whose goal is to recruit a Referral Source, Trudy Grossman, who might help him secure a radio talk show interview with her friend Ethel Clearchannel to promote his new book. Here is how a potential contact could play out:

Greeting: "Hi, Trudy."

Small talk: "How are you doing? . . . How's your family? . . . Did you go anywhere over the weekend?"

Purpose: "Trudy, the reason I'm calling is to see if you can help me get a radio talk show interview to promote my new book. And I'd also like to show you how I can help you generate referrals for your business. Right now I'd like to give you a quick overview of some ideas I have and get your reaction to them. Is this a good time? If you're interested, we can arrange to discuss them later in more detail." (If yes, continue.)

Overview: "As I'm sure you know, getting referrals is one of the best ways to generate business. I've been reading about a systematic approach for generating referrals that was developed by Dr. Ivan Misner and Mike Macedonio, and I've prepared a plan that will help me attract more customers and business opportunities. It's practical, and I believe it covers everything. If you're interested, I'd like to show you how to use the system for your business, too. Are you interested?" (If yes, continue.)

Scheduling the meeting: "Great! I'd like to meet with you as soon as possible — say, within the next week or two — to tell you my ideas. It should take about an hour. When would be the best time for you?"

Close: "Okay, Trudy, I'll send you an outline of what we need to discuss and some information that will help you understand how the system works. You should get it in a day or two. If you have any questions before we meet, please don't hesitate to call. It was great talking with you. I look forward to our meeting on _____ at _____."

Completing the First Phase

Based on the guidelines and sample script, develop an outline that you can use for your initial contact with your prospective sources. After you've reviewed the remaining four phases of this activation process, you can fine tune your script and begin making calls.

Finding the "Sweet Spot" of Referral Partners

As we have gone through this book we have been giving you different referral relationships to help build your business. As your referral marketing plan becomes more refined, you will start to identify and build relationships with people who can significantly impact your referral success. In many cases we find that these special referral relationships are with what we call 'referral partners.' These would be the referral relationship that meets all six criteria *and* have a Profitability level relationship with you. These are the people that are in 'the sweet spot.'

By using the diagram below, you can see how the concentric circles represent referral opportunities. On the outer circle are Referral Sources. In Chapter 13, we identified the eight sources of referrals. These are all the people that could refer you.

The circle inside of that contains the Contact Sphere professionals. As mentioned previously, Contact Spheres are a group of business professions that complement, rather than compete with, your business.

The next circle includes a group we mentioned first in Chapter 13, the Power Team. Your Power Team includes the people with whom you have a relationship, are in your Contact Sphere, and with whom you are actively engaging in a Referral relationship.

Finally, we have the Referral Partners, who meet all six criteria of a Referral Source. With only a few Referral Partners meeting all six criteria and with a developed relationship operating in P on the VCP Process®, most business owners can notice remarkable referrals. This is another area in referral marketing that is 'simple but not easy' to attain. However, by having the sweet spot as your focus, you can recruit the right referral relationships.

Referral Network

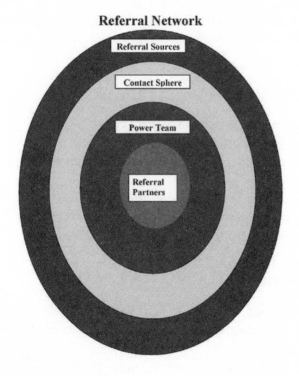

Eight Sources of Referrals

1. Contact sphere
2. Clients

3. People whose business benefits when yours does
4. Networking groups
5. People you do business with
6. Staff
7. People you give referrals
8. Anyone who has given you referrals

Contact Spheres

A Contact Sphere is a group of business professions that complement, rather than compete with, your business.

Power Teams

The people with whom you have a relationship with are in your Contact Sphere, and you are actively engaging in a Referral relationship.

Referral Partners

Those who meet the six criteria of a Referral Source:

1. Want, or can be inspired to, help you;
2. Have time, or are willing to make the time, to help you;
3. Have the ability, or can be trained to do, the things you want them to do;
4. Have the resources necessary to help you;
5. Have relationships with the types of people you want to target; and
6. Will make good referrals for people you know.

⇒ *Action Items*

1. List the people who are in your Power Team
2. List your network members that meet all six criteria of a Referral Source.
3. List the people in your referral network that have the possibility to be Referral Partners.
4. Meet with these people to discuss the opportunity to be Referral Partners.

21

Briefing Your Sources

Training Your Network Members to Send Referrals

Upon getting a business referral, Mr. John Q. Businessman simply takes down the name and contact information of the potential customer, Arlene D. Prospect, from the Referral Source. Sometime later, he calls the prospect and introduces himself: "Hello, Ms. Prospect, my name is John Businessman. Larry Source recommended I call you. I'm an accountant. . . ."

Handling referrals this way, as you might expect, gets minimal results. Your chance of converting the referral into a customer will be greater if your Referral Source helps by doing the following:

- Makes the initial contact with the prospect (his acquaintance) to assess her need and, if appropriate, alert her that you will be getting in touch
- Sends the prospect background information about you and your business
- Lets the prospect know the nature of his relationship with you
- Gives the prospect a brief description and endorsement of your products or services
- Arranges to introduce the prospect to you
- Follows up with the prospect after you contact her

Unfortunately, if you don't ask your prospective Referral Source to do some of these things, he probably won't — not because he isn't willing, but because he doesn't know these actions could make a big difference, doesn't have enough information about you or your business, or simply doesn't know how.

A Plan for Your Source

There are two main actions you need to take:

1. Communicate to your sources the actions you wish them to take.
2. Provide them with all materials necessary to accomplish those actions.

More specifically, it is your responsibility to your prospective Referral Sources to —

- prepare an agenda for a briefing session
- show them how they can help you generate referrals and convert them into customers
- develop sample correspondence and literature for them
- prepare outlines and scripts that they can use when making contact with prospects
- give them clear instructions on what you want them to do for you
- provide typing and other administrative support
- pay all expenses they incur on your behalf, including postage, telephone calls, and promotional materials
- make it as easy as possible for them to support you

Exactly how do you meet these responsibilities? There are four steps to briefing a prospective Referral Source:

Step 1:

When you make your first call asking for help, give your prospective Referral Source a brief overview of your approach to getting referrals.

Step 2:

Before your first meeting, send your prospective source a packet of information and materials (as you promised in your phone call), including

- a comprehensive agenda for the briefing session
- a description of the source's role and yours
- sample outlines, scripts, and other materials

You should call before your first meeting to be sure your prospective source has received these materials. Remind him to take a look at the materials. You can do this by asking whether he has any questions about them. Your training session will go faster and more smoothly if he has read the materials ahead of time.

Step 3:

Conduct Referral Source education and training. Each session can be formal or informal, a one-on-one meeting, or a class lesson for several sources at once, whatever fits your situation, your style, and your prospective sources' needs. For at least the first session, you should be the person conducting the training. Later, you may find that some of your better Referral Sources can be very effective in helping you train new sources. The responsibility for all training costs is yours, of course.

This step, briefing your Prospective Sources, is the heart of the process — don't do it haphazardly. Your goal is to teach your sources how to carry out the roles they will play in helping you generate referrals and convert them into customers.

Sample Agenda

Introduction
Thanks
Purpose of meeting:

- Explain how you can help me generate referrals and convert them into clients
- Teach you what you need to know to act as a Referral Source
- Provide the tools you need to carry out your role as a Referral Source
- Finalize a plan of action

Overview of agenda
Review of support materials mailed
Business development goals:

- Overview of my products and services
- Target market

Benefits to be gained
Advantages of using the five-phase system
How the five-phase system works:

- Definitions
- Prerequisites
- The five phases

Other ways to provide support
How the system can be used to help you
Recommended plan of action
Questions and answers
Finalization of action plan
Conclusion

Roles

My role (partial list)

Before the meeting:
- Select target market
- Identify desired help

During meeting:
- Develop and provide training for you
- Provide you with complimentary samples of products and services

After meeting:
- Provide you with required support materials and funds to pay for all expenses, including postage and telephone calls

Your role (partial list)

- Collect and provide information about prospects
- Contact prospect before contacting me
- Give prospect background information and promote my products and services
- Send information packet to prospect

Review with your source the materials you sent. Be thorough and quick. Try to limit your training to an hour or two. If you need more time, spread it over several days. The more your Referral Sources know about you, your business, and what they can do to assist you, the better — but don't use up too much of their valuable time.

To train her referral resources, Dawn Lyons, Vice President and Partner of the Referral Institute, conducted an evening session at a BNI Conference. The BNI Directors attending the conference are Referral Institute's best Referral Sources to find trainers and coaches to start up the Referral Institute in their areas. During the information session, which lasted about two hours and was attended by over 100 Directors, Dawn gave participants the following information:

- a description of the programs the Referral Institute was offering
- a list of ways they could help her
- a list of ways Referral Institute can help BNI

The sessions were a major success. They were a great way for Dawn to get the support she needed and to increase her Referral Sources' awareness of her organization and how they could contribute to its success. She plans to offer another session at the upcoming International and National Conferences.

Step 4:

Provide the Referral Source with follow-up materials, information, and support as needed. Continue the training via telephone conversations and additional briefings and debriefings, especially after his first few calls to prospects. This will enable your Referral Sources to:

- help you collect key information that you could not have obtained on your own
- better understand your products or services and communicate their value to others
- answer key questions about you and your products or services

Right now you're probably thinking: '*Whoa, I could never expect my Referral Sources to do all these things for me. A sit-down training session would take much more time than they have available, and the amount of work I'm asking them to do would make them feel like unpaid employees.*'

Remember the conditions we set earlier: This process applies only to people with whom you have a long, strong relationship, a high level of trust, or an agreement to perform services for each other for your mutual benefit. In effect, these people are informal business partners with you;

you have agreed to perform unpaid services for each other that will help your respective businesses. Often this informal agreement has been made in an organizational setting, such as a referral service organization.

If it has not already been explicitly agreed to, tell your prospective source that you wish to share with him the process you are using to generate referral business. Tell him exactly what you are doing, in terms of both your business mission and the means you use to obtain new customers, and that you wish to learn the same things about his business. The results you expect are twofold:

1. He will send you new referral business.
2. He will improve his referral-generating process and get referral business from you.

The Short Course

You will find yourself in many relationships that fall short of the close, trusting kind needed for the formal training sessions described above. In fact, you may get occasional referrals from people you haven't even met. Between these extremes, however, is a broad range of relationships that call for different ways of imparting information about yourself and your products or services that can be passed along to prospects. Many of the motivational tactics outlined also serve, in part, as a form of training for your Referral Source.

Here are several ways, both formal and informal, to provide your sources useful information about your products or services, information they can pass along to prospects that may result in referral business:

- Ask your prospective source to critique your marketing materials, such as your flyers, brochures, videos, audiotapes, even your résumé. Send them your drafts, not the finished product. As they offer advice on how to improve the item, they will learn more about your business and remember more facts about you.
- Send them your newsletter. In it you can describe activities your sources may not be familiar with. They can pass this information, or even the entire newsletter, to people who might want to do business with you.

- Ask your source to introduce you for a presentation you are going to make. Your source will want more information about you in order to make a good introduction. Promise to help her by providing her with notes.
- Tell your friends and associates, especially new ones, you want to get to know them better. Ask for information about their jobs, professions, interests, organizations, networks, and hobbies. At the same time, give them a profile of yourself, including a picture to inform those you haven't seen what you look like.
- Invite your sources to attend events at which they can learn more about you — an award ceremony, an open house, a trade show, or a social function. Make sure they learn something about you from the invitation itself. If you sponsor the event but are not the main attraction, try to devote a few minutes after the main presentation to describing your business. Financial consultants often sponsor lunchtime speakers and use the opportunity for an additional brief presentation of their services.
- Record information about yourself in your answering machine message. One businessman uses this message: "Thanks for calling Chesney Communications. We produce the business television program 'Windows on Wall Street.' If you're calling about our duplication services, press 22; our video production services, press 30; for all other departments, press 0."
- Invite a source to speak to your group about something she does or knows. This will lead her to ask for facts about you and your organization.
- Invite sources to visit your web page. Send them a note announcing your new web page and ask them to provide feedback. Make sure it offers information that will help them understand your business.
- At the end of your email messages, after your name include a "sig" file that lists information such as nicknames, positions you hold, books you've written, and special recognition you've received. Limit your list to 10 lines. Change your sig periodically so that regular correspondents can learn more about you.
- Ask your source for advice. Give him plenty of background information to help him formulate his recommendations.

Here is Mike's email "sig" as an example of helpful information to include in an email signature:

Mike Macedonio
New York Times Best Selling Author
President & Partner Referral Institute
Creating Referrals For Life®
707-780-8110 Office
www.referralinstitute.com
mikem@referralinstitute.com

   The Referral Institute is proud to announce our selection as one of the top 500 rated franchises in Entrepreneur's Annual Franchise 500 for five years in a row.

Getting to Know You

As we learned in the GAINS approach, getting acquainted with your sources is a two-way street. You need to know about your prospective source in order to gauge the kind of prospect she is likely to send you and work within the framework of her business or profession. She needs to know about you in order to select good prospects for your products or services and to recommend your strengths and specialties to them.

   When the benefits come through, it's still a two-way street. Make sure the source of a good referral can benefit from your actions in return for her help to you. There are several ways of accomplishing this, as you will see in later chapters.

⇒ *Action Items*

Brief a prospective Referral Source using the four-step process:

Step 1: Make your first call asking for help; give your prospective Referral Source a brief overview of your approach to getting referrals.

Step 2: Send your prospective source a packet of information and materials (as you should promise to do in your phone call), including:

- comprehensive agenda for the briefing session
- description of the source's role and yours
- sample outlines, scripts, and other materials

Step 3: Conduct Referral Source education and training.
Step 4: Provide the Referral Source with follow-up materials, information, and support, as needed.

22

Priming Your Prospects

Your Source's First Contact on Your Behalf

The third phase of activating your referral network has the most significant impact on your success in converting referrals into customers — and it's the only action in the process that's not yours to take. It is your Referral Source's responsibility to make the first contact with your prospect (her acquaintance) to tell him he'll be hearing from you. There's a good reason for this: The prospect is more likely to talk with you, purchase your product or service, or provide a business opportunity if he learns about you from someone he trusts.

He's even more likely to do so if your source first does a little research into whether he might need, want, or be interested in your product or service. If your Referral Source learns that the prospect can benefit from your business, she tells him about you; if not, she simply doesn't mention you.

Be Inquisitive

Perhaps the best way for your source to assess the prospect is to ask questions, and she's usually better positioned to get the answers than you are. Using the example we introduced in Chapter 20, Dr. Star's Referral Source, Trudy Grossman, can ask the prospect (her friend Ethel Clearchannel, the radio show host) questions such as these:

- How do you select guests for your show? Who makes the final decision?
- What kind of topics do you like to cover?
- What topics do you plan to cover during the next few months?
- Are you open to suggestions? Would you be interested in some referrals?
- What dates are you trying to fill?

Once your source tells you how the prospect responded to her questions, you'll have a better idea of how to approach her when your turn comes. Then, when the time is right and circumstances are favorable, ask your source to alert the prospect that you'll be getting in touch.

Follow Through

After your source talks with the prospect, she should follow up in writing. This gives the prospect an opportunity to learn more about you before you make contact — or serves as a reminder if the prospect has forgotten what the source said about you. This follow-up should include a cover letter and some brochures or other literature describing your background and business — materials that you have thoughtfully provided your source (in the second phase).

Here's an example of a follow-up letter from a Referral Source to a prospect — in this case, Dr. Mark Star's source Trudy Grossman, to her friend Ethel, the talk show host:

January 3, 2011

Hi, Ethel,

It was great talking with you. Congratulations on your nomination for VP of your community organization. I am delighted that things are going well with you.

The materials I promised to send you on Dr. Mark Star are enclosed. As I mentioned, Mark would be an excellent guest for your show. He recently appeared on "Making It" on KYPA and talked about strategies for achieving goals. As usual, Mark was lively, professional, and very informative. Here's a copy of his brochure for your review.

If you have no objections, I will ask Mark to give you a call next week.

See you at the breakfast meeting next month.

Trudy Grossman

cc: Dr. Mark Star

Provide Feedback

Finally, the Referral Source should let you know what's happened. She can do this by phone, email, fax, or other means, or, as in the above example, by forwarding to you a copy of her letter to the prospect. Make sure she lets you know who is expected to make the next move, and when.

This may seem like a lot to ask of a Referral Source, but remember, you are handling most of the behind-the-scenes work that makes the system effective. In addition, your Referral Source derives several benefits from helping you:

- The opportunity to contact an acquaintance for reasons other than her own business needs.
- A stronger relationship with the prospect.
- A chance to look like a hero for offering a referral with no expectation of monetary reward.
- A commitment from you, the vendor, to reciprocate by helping her secure referrals for her business.
- Being viewed as a source.

Thus, getting support from a Referral Source works in the best interests of both of you. More important, working with your Referral Source will yield far greater results than working alone.

23

Asking for Referrals and Contacting Your Prospects

Follow This Action Plan to Make it Happen

Has someone you didn't even know ever solicited you for a referral or for business? Michelle Villalobos, a BNI member in Miami, calls this *"Premature Solicitation."* (Say that fast three times, and you might get in trouble!)

We agree completely with Michelle. In fact, we've each been victims of "premature solicitation" many times.

I was recently speaking at a business networking event and, before my presentation, someone literally came up to me and said, "Hi, it is a real pleasure to meet you. I understand you know Richard Branson. I offer specialized marketing services and I am sure his Virgin enterprises could benefit from what I provide. Could you please introduce me to him so that I can show him how this would assist his companies?"

OK, so what I was thinking was:

Are you completely insane? I'm going to introduce you, someone I don't know and don't have any relationship with, to Sir Richard, whom I've only met a few times, so that you can proceed to attempt to sell him a product or service that I don't know anything about and haven't used myself? Yeah, right. That's NEVER going to happen.

I am pleased to report, however, that with much effort, I was able to keep that little monologue inside my own head, opting instead for a much more subtle response.

I replied . . . "Hi, I'm Ivan, I'm sorry—I don't think we've met before, what was your name again?" That surprised the man enough to make him realize that his "solicitation" might have been a bit "premature." I explained that I regularly refer people to my contacts, but only after I've established a long-term strong relationship with the service provider first. He said thanks and moved on to his next victim.

— DR. IVAN MISNER

Networking is not about hunting. It is about farming — it's about cultivating relationships. Don't engage in "premature solicitation." You'll be a better networker if you remember that.

Every time we start to think there must surely be an almost universal feeling of distaste for that approach to networking, we are brought back to reality by the minority of people who still think that this is actually a good networking technique.

To our astonishment, someone once actually wrote the following in an online comment to an article Ivan wrote for Entrepreneur.com:

"I don't happen to believe that you need a relationship with the person you are asking first. What you must have is a compelling story or product/service that would genuinely benefit the referral . . .

The fact that you had not cultivated a relationship with the person has become irrelevant because, more importantly, you had been in a position to help [your contact] benefit from the introduction. If it's of genuine benefit to the person being referred, I don't see the problem . . .

It's about the benefit of what's being referred rather than the relationship with the person asking for the referral . . .

Who am I to deny my contacts something good?"

Wow. What can we say? So "the relationship" is irrelevant?! All you have to have is a good story, product, or service; tell folks about it; and those people owe it to you (who may be literally a stranger to them) to introduce you to a good contact of theirs! Really? People really think this way!? According to the writer of the comments above, it doesn't matter if I actually know or *trust* the person wanting the business. As long as the person has a good product (or so he says), we should refer that person because we would "deny" my contacts "something good!"

Ask and You Shall Receive . . .
We do believe that in order to get referrals you need to ask for them. The key, however, is to know how to ask and when it is appropriate to make the request. When is the right time, you ask? The right time to ask for a referral is when BOTH parties are in the Credibility phase of the referral relationship. Networking should not be a system that ends up alienating your friends and family. Be conscious of the deposits you make into your relationships before you start writing checks or, in essence, *asking* for referrals from those with whom you have relationships.

Networkers Against Premature Solicitation — unite! We need to teach people that this is *not* a good way to network!

Five-Step Action Plan for Building on the Introduction from Your Referral Source

1. Your First Communication with Your Future Client

Your Referral Source has done her job. Now it's time to contact the prospect. But be careful: the purpose of your first contact is not to make a sale or even to ask the prospect if he has questions about your business. You should only present your products or services during this contact if the prospect asks!

The purpose of the initial contact with the prospect is to:

- Begin to build the relationship
- Get to know the prospect better
- Help the prospect get to know you better
- Position yourself to make your next contact
- See if the prospect fits your source's description

Before making contact, do your homework. If you don't have them, ask for copies of all correspondence your source sent the prospect on your behalf. Find out from your source the best way to make your initial contact: telephone? letter? Email?

2. Meet the Face

When your source gives you the green light, don't let the opportunity grow stale. Make your first contact with the prospect within 72 hours. If your source can be present, the most advantageous way is a face-to-face meeting in which your source can introduce you. This introduction should be more than just, "Harry, this is Jerry. Jerry, this is Harry." Your source should give the prospect a more thorough briefing about you, your business, and your products or services. For example:

"Harry Prospect, this is Vic Vendor, whom I was telling you about last week at our club meeting. Vic and I have known each other for more than five years. For the last two years, I've let him handle all my travel arrangements, and I can't count up all the money he's saved me, not to mention bench time in airport lounges. Vic's really active in the community: we're going to give him our service award at our next chamber meeting. He's also a good golfer, and he skis a lot in the winter, although I find that hard to believe because he's never broken a leg!"

"Vic, Harry has been a very special customer of mine for at least 15 years. His daughter and mine went to school together, and he let me cater her wedding three years ago . . ." And so forth.

During your first contact, the prospect will be watching to see whether you are as enthusiastic, caring, articulate, straightforward, and intelligent as your source said you were. He may have questions, but typically will not ask them during the first meeting unless he has an urgent need for the kind of products or services you provide.

3. Drop a Line

If your first meeting with your prospect can't be in person, your best bet is to write — a letter, a card, or email, for example — rather than to phone, as you did your prospective source. Writing gives you a better, more controlled opportunity to convey what you've learned about the prospect. It helps develop your relationship to let your prospect know you find him interesting enough to have taken the time to learn a few facts about him — not the fact that he needs your products or services, but the fact that he's a member of the Downtown Executive Society, or that, "Tom told me you're a great chess player." Express an interest in meeting him. Advise him that you'll be calling to schedule a mutually convenient appointment. Don't expect him to have read, or to remember, the materials your source sent him.

Start by naming your Referral Source — a name he will recognize. For example:

Dear Glen:

Joan Irvine, who I understand was one of your students, recommended that I get in touch with you. Joan tells me that you are an avid butterfly collector . . .

Don't send business literature or your card with your first correspondence. Your stationery should have all the contact information your prospect needs to reach you. Avoid giving the impression that you are interested in him primarily as a prospective customer.

If your prospect will agree, schedule a meeting. Regardless, offer to send more information, and if the prospect indicates he would like this, do so right away (and don't forget to send a copy of your correspondence to your Referral Source).

4. Time for the Telephone

If your source recommends it and can guide you as to the best time to do so, you can contact your prospect by telephone:

"Hello, Ms. Clearchannel, I'm Dr. Mark Star, and I'm calling you at the recommendation of Trudy Grossman."

"Oh, hi, Mark. Trudy told me about you. She's quite impressed with your book. I'd like to have you on my show. Can you come to my studio two weeks from today?"

The above situation could happen, of course: the prospect could decide immediately to do business with you. If you've prepared the ground well, and if you're lucky, your efforts may pay off on your very first call. Most often, though, the prospect, even a referred lead, will need more time or will express an interest in talking later about your products or services. However, you're almost certainly better off than if you made your first contact by cold call, mass advertising, or direct-mail campaign.

5. Follow Up

When building relationships, it's always important not to let much time lapse without following up the first contact. Within 72 hours, send your prospect a note expressing your pleasure in communicating with her. It's still too early, though, to send business literature or make any move toward sales promotion.

Follow up early, but don't push beyond the prospect's comfort level. Once the prospect has expressed an interest in your products or services, provide information about them, but don't force it on her. Continue presenting your products or services, but avoid the hard sell. Focus on fulfilling her needs and interests. Your goal should be to keep your prospect aware of your business without annoying her.

Remember, to secure the long-term loyalty of your prospect and convert her into a customer, you must first build a relationship, and that relationship must develop through the Visibility, Credibility, and Profitability stages. It may take a while, but if you've selected and briefed your sources well, and if you use the above five-step action plan to its best advantage, you'll speed up the process.

24

Recognizing and Rewarding Your Sources

Providing Feedback and Incentives to Your Network Members

The final phase in activating your referral network is to keep your Referral Source in the loop of anything that has happened since she gave you the referral, and to show your appreciation. It's important to recognize and reward your source, both before and certainly after a referral has become a customer. This chapter will show you how to set up two important parts of this process: a system for sharing results and a system for recognizing and rewarding Referral Sources.

Share Results

Be sure to share your results regularly and systematically with your Referral Sources. First, determine the kinds of information about results you want to share, and then set up a method of capturing this information. It should come from the data you have collected in your Relate2Profit database or other contact management system. If it doesn't, modify the form. Next, determine how you will share the results — that is, by phone, email, fax, card, or letter. Whatever the means, always do the following:

- give your Referral Source a brief update on what has happened.
- share what you plan to do next.
- promise to keep her informed.

This third point is important. You want your Referral Source to expect to hear from you regularly. Your promise sets up that expectation; it obligates you to keep in touch, and you must keep your promises. Your relationship must develop beyond Visibility into Credibility before you can expect to reach Profitability. You can reinforce your Credibility by saying, "I promised to keep you informed of my situation, so here's my news." But remember: failure to keep this promise will damage the relationship you have worked so hard to build.

To reinforce the relationship, call or write your source to talk about something other than the prospect. Pass along news about your personal or professional life and ask about hers. Now and then, send a small, thoughtful gift or complimentary offering — an inspirational message, a product sample, an article, or perhaps a piece of your newest literature.

You will derive many benefits from sharing your results with your Referral Source. Doing so will:

- increase your likelihood of getting additional support. Informing your source of your plans gives her an opportunity to support or advise you and keeps the information pipeline open.
- keep your name in front of the prospect and your Referral Source, keep your source and prospect in touch with each other, and increase your chances of being remembered by both. You can bet that when your Referral Source and prospect get together, they will talk about your situation.
- strengthen your relationship with the Referral Source because each update includes yet another expression of gratitude. People like to be thought of as helpful.
- enhance your source's knowledge of you and your business. Sharing your results contributes to her education, increasing her confidence in you and her ability to spot prospective customers for your business.

Create a Reward Program

To share rewards equitably and effectively, you must do so *predictably*. This requires being explicit and systematic in your reward philosophy. If you reward certain actions only some of the time, your sources will consider you ungrateful or unreliable. To establish a consistent reward program that provides incentive for your sources, you need to decide:

- When to reward a source — upon receipt of a good referral. Recognition should be given to all qualified referrals, not just the ones that close. You're recognizing the Referral Sources efforts, not your ability to close the deal or the prospect's capacity to buy.

- What kind of reward — reference your GAINS on your Referral Source to find out what they would like. Be careful of finder's fees. If a referred prospect found out about a finder's fee arrangement, this could taint the referral. It may also hurt the relationship between the Referral Source and the prospect, as well as the prospect and you.
- How much you can afford — what's the best gift you can offer within your budget?
- What kind of reward your sources would value most — and probably not buy for themselves? Again, your GAINS research will provide valuable insight.
- When and how the reward will be presented.

We will cover rewards and incentive programs in much greater detail in Chapter 28.

⇒ *Action Items*

1. Track the source of all business opportunities in Relate2Profit or other contact management system.
2. Have a system to recognize each referred business opportunity.

25

Budgeting for Referrals
Allocating Your Time and Your Money

Systematic referral marketing requires planning. You need to budget the time and money you'll need for your referral marketing. In this chapter we will outline a step-by-step approach you can use, and several considerations you need to be aware of, in budgeting your time. Then we will describe a similar approach for your expenses.

Budgeting and Allocating Your Time

Every business plan should include estimates of how long it will take and how the time will be used. Before implementing your referral marketing plan, check to see if you will have enough time to carry out your plans. If you don't have this information, you risk the following:

- spending too much or too little time on a particular effort
- losing control of your time
- realizing little or no return on your investment of time
- abandoning your efforts too soon

In our systematic approach to budgeting time, we've identified seven steps.

(NOTE: This system is for those interested in a step-by-step budgeting approach. If this isn't you, you can skip this section.)

All that you need to do to complete component 8 of your referral marketing plan is the first two steps; you'll also need to do step 7 to schedule contacts on your master calendar (component 9). If you prefer a more detailed approach, you can do steps 3 through 6 as well.

Step 1: Estimate Total Time Available

Your campaign can be as long as you want it to be — three, six, nine, twelve months or more. Within those constraints, how much time do you wish to devote to your referral marketing? Will you need 100, 200, 350, or 500 hours? The time you have available, that you reserve, will determine the nature and quality of your referral marketing by influencing your selection of tactics, objectives, resources, targets, and so forth.

To estimate the time you will need, use whatever information you can from your past experience and the experiences of others, such as your network members. About how much time did you spend last year on developing relationships and networking? If no such information is available, make an educated guess for your first campaign, then adjust using this initial experience as a guide.

Your time estimate can be a daily, weekly, monthly, quarterly, or annual figure. Our example will span 12 months, and we will allocate 120 hours to our six selected Referral Sources.

Step 2: Estimate Total Time Available per Period

Allocate the available time — 120 hours in our example — by month. Let's assume our business is seasonal and that we will have less time available for networking in the summer and the holiday season.

Month

1	2	3	4	5	6	7	8	9	10	11	12

Hrs.

12	12	12	12	10	8	8	8	12	12	8	6

For a more detailed approach to budgeting your time, complete steps 3–6. Otherwise, move ahead to step 7 and plan your calendar.

Step 3: Allocate Time per Source

Allocate part of the total available time to each source. In our example, we have 120 hours available for six sources this year. We can allocate 20 hours to each — or, more realistically, we can apportion it unevenly, depending on how important we consider each source:

Referral Source	Total Hours Available
No. 1	30
No. 2	20
No. 3	25
No. 4	15
No. 5	20
No. 6	10
Total	120

We recommend that you budget for no more than 10 individuals the first time around. As you develop and refine your system, you can expand your network of Referral Sources.

Step 4: Determine the Number of Contacts per Source

Taking into consideration the total time you allocated to each Referral Source in step 3, decide how many times you wish to contact each source during the campaign. Classify each as a daily, weekly, monthly, quarterly, semiannual, or other target. Sources you contact less than twice a year cannot truly be considered primary Referral Sources.

Referral Source	Total Hours Available	Contacts per Campaign
No. 1	30	24 (twice per month)
No. 2	20	12 (monthly)
No. 3	25	17 (every third week)
No. 4	15	12 (monthly)
No. 5	20	12 (monthly)
No. 6	10	6 (every other month)
Total	120	

Step 5: Determine the Length of Each Contact

Distribute the time you assigned each target in step 3 among the contacts you identified in step 4. For example, you allocated 30 hours to source number one for the 12-month period, and you will make 24 contacts. How much of the 30 hours should you allocate to each of the 24 contacts? It's unlikely that you would distribute the time evenly, with each meeting lasting an hour and a quarter. For simplicity, make 18 of the contacts one hour each, and give two hours to each of the other six contacts.

Referral Source	Total Hours Available	Contacts per Campaign
No. 1	30	*24 (18 @ 1.0h; 6 @ 2.0h)*
No. 2	20	*12 (8 @ 1.5h; 4 @ 2.0h)*
No. 3	25	*17 (9 @ 1.0h; 8 @ 2.0h)*
No. 4	15	*12 (9 @ 1.0h; 3 @ 2.0h)*
No. 5	20	*12 (8 @ 1.5h; 4 @ 2.0h)*
No. 6	10	*6 (4 @ 1.5h; 2 @ 2.0h)*
Total	120	

Scheduling Tactics

How many contacts should you make? How often should you make them? Here are several ways to answer these questions and speed the process of developing effective, rewarding relationships.

1. Spread out your contacts. Regardless of the level of your relationship, the more contacts you can make with a source, the better. Two short meetings are more beneficial than one long session. Each meeting becomes an opportunity to strengthen the relationship, to move it along, to enhance your visibility and for recognition. Your targets will remember you better.

2. Schedule predictably. Stay in contact with your targets regularly and consistently; train them to expect to hear from you at certain times. This tactic builds positive expectancy. For example, if you usually contact one of your sources during the first week of every quarter, she will come to expect it and will budget time for you. If she doesn't hear from you, she may call to see if something is wrong.

3. Link new contact activities with established ones. Getting into new routines is not easy, but one of the fastest and surest ways to establish good habits is to link them with old habits.

4. Make each contact lead to the next. Before concluding a meeting or telephone conversation, schedule the date of your next contact. In written correspondence, close by stating the date your target should expect to hear from you again: "I'll send you a note within 45 days." Having made the commitment, you're more likely to follow through. This practice establishes a chain of contacts, with each meeting leading to the next.

5. Assume responsibility for making contact. You can't control whether a source will contact you when you need help; you can control only what you do yourself. Take the initiative; stay in touch with your source.

6. Stick to your plan. As your referral marketing achieves success and you establish routines with your sources, some of them may begin taking the contact initiative. Don't let these contacts interfere with your contact schedule; that is, don't count contacts they initiate as fulfillment of the contacts you've scheduled. By keeping to your schedule, you can subtly condition your Referral Sources and keep your plan on track.

Step 6: Determine the Time per Activity

In implementing your referral marketing plan, you will use your time in any or all of six activities:

Activity	Description
1. Assessing	Researching and determining needs
2. Planning	Decision making, forecasting, budgeting, and scheduling
3. Preparing	Developing tools and resources — including training — needed to carry out your plan of action
4. Implementing	Actions needed to achieve your goals: meetings, presentations, telephone calls, or letters
5. Evaluating	Tracking and evaluating results
6. Other	All other activities

The time you reserved in step 5 for each contact will be used performing one or more of these activities. For example, if you allocated two hours to make your first contact with source number one, you might assign 20 minutes to each of the six activities — 20 minutes for assessing, 20 minutes for planning, 20 minutes for preparing, and so on. It's more likely, however, that these activities will require different amounts of time. Your first contact might require 30 minutes of assessing, 45 minutes of planning, 15 minutes of preparing, and 30 minutes of implementing.

Step 7: Set Up Your Calendar

When you've finished budgeting your time in a manner that you consider practical and achievable, set a target date for each contact on your referral marketing plan. Add all other primary relationship development and referral marketing activities to this calendar, including the activities detailed in the forecasting and evaluation chapters that follow.

Budgeting and Allocating Your Costs

Systematic relationship development and referral marketing also requires you to estimate the cost of your activities. The steps involved are similar to those in budgeting your time. The first two are enough for a good general approach to estimating your costs, and they are all that you need to do to complete the 10th component of your referral marketing plan. If you prefer a more detailed approach, continue with steps 3–6.

Step 1: Estimate Total Funds Available

Because the amount of money you have available will limit your marketing activities, don't implement your referral marketing until you've budgeted your costs. First, do one of two things:

- Determine how much you have to spend, and then select tactics you can use within those limitations; or
- Plot what you would like to do, and then establish a budget that will cover your costs.

For our example, we will use the latter approach and plan a 12-month campaign with $5,400 total funds available for six prospective Referral Sources.

In real life, you'll have to decide on a total budget based on experience. Start with an estimate, an educated guess.

- How much can you spare?
- How much do your network members spend?
- How much will you need to accomplish the activities you planned in your calendar?
- How much did you spend last year on similar activities — seminars, networking associations, or business lunches?

Try to dedicate at least as much for your first referral marketing plan. By channeling the money toward a specific purpose — increasing your referral business — you'll be making it work a lot more effectively than before.

All that's required now is to allocate your money over the period of your referral marketing (step 2). However, if you complete steps 3–6, you'll get a better idea of whether the figure you chose is a good estimate. If it isn't, raise or lower it and run through the steps again, repeating the exercise until you have a budget that works.

Step 2: Estimate Total Funds Available per Period

Allocate the available funds, $5,400, by month. We'll distribute our funds the same way we distributed our time, weighted seasonally:

Month

1	2	3	4	5	6	7	8	9	10	11	12
$											
490	490	490	490	450	410	410	410	490	490	410	370

For a more detailed approach to budgeting your expenses, complete the next four steps. Otherwise, move ahead to Chapter 26, "Forecasting Sales from Referrals."

Step 3: Determine the Funding Amount per Source

Having reserved $5,400 for our six selected Referral Sources, we will now decide how much money we'll need for each source. We could allocate the money equally, but since we're going to spend more time with some sources than with others, we should probably allocate the money more or less proportionately.

Referral Source	Funds Available
No. 1	$1,100
No. 2	$1,000
No. 3	$1,100
No. 4	$800
No. 5	$900
No. 6	$800
Total	$5,400

Step 4: Determine the Number of Contacts per Source

If this step sounds familiar, it should. It's the same fourth step you used to budget your referral marketing time. Use the figures you've already decided on.

Step 5: Determine the Funding per Contact

How much will you spend on each contact? In our example, we allocated $1,000 to source number three. We're going to meet 17 times with this source — Nine one-hour contacts and eight two-hour contacts. How do we divide the $1,000 among these 17 contacts? Here's one way:

Contact Length	Cost per Contact x	No. of Contacts =	Total
1 hour	$40	9	$360
2 hours	$80	8	$640
Totals		17	$1,000

Continue by deciding which contacts will be one-hour contacts and which will be two-hour contacts. For example, you might find it advantageous to start with a two-hour meeting to discuss your proposal at length with your source. If so, contact number one with this source will show a distribution of $80 among expense categories.

Step 6: Determine Funding per Expense Category

Implementing your referral marketing plan will involve a variety of expenses. We've identified 14 expense categories that will apply to most referral marketing plans; you can add or delete categories to fit your circumstances.

Expense Categories

1. Contributions/gifts/donations/sponsorships
2. Copying/printing/developing & processing
3. Entertainment
4. Facilities rental
5. Meals
6. Membership fees
7. Postage
8. Subscriptions
9. Self-development
10. Service fees/professional/consulting
11. Supplies & equipment
12. Telephone/fax/email
13. Travel (mileage, hotel, parking, taxi, etc.)
14. Other

⇛ *Action Items*

1. Download a free referral marketing plan template from www. referralinstitute.com/WBKMS. Once you have set up a user account, use the coupon code WBKMS to receive your referral marketing plan template.
2. Review your action items from the previous chapters.
3. Document these action items into your referral marketing plan.
4. Allocate the money you set aside for each contact (step 5) among these expense categories.

26

Forecasting Sales from Referrals
Watching the Road Ahead

By this point you should have a pretty good idea of the shape and composition of your business and your network, how you are going to use your network, and how much time and money your referral marketing will cost you. The next step is to look down the road a bit and set goals.

To set realistic goals, however, you must first answer the following questions:

- How do you expect your business to change as a result of your referral marketing?
- How many referrals do you expect to get?
- What dollar value do you expect to realize from these referrals?
- How many Referral Sources will you need to achieve these projections?

You could guess at the answers to these questions, but there's a better way: You can utilize a systematic method of setting your goals using your experience as a base. First, look back at a recent period of sales revenues from referrals and all other sources (your reference period). Then project what you expect revenue to be as a result of your referral marketing (your first forecast). Your forecast should be based on four factors:

1. The number of referrals you expect to receive
2. The dollar value of the referrals you expect to get
3. The percentage of your business you expect to result from referrals
4. The number of sources you will need to achieve the expected number and dollar value of referrals

Analyzing Your Reference Period

The first thing you need to do is to analyze these four factors during a recent business period — use this as your reference period. One year is usually the standard. If you've been in business less than a year or do not have 12 months of data to analyze, you may use a shorter period of time, such as three, six, or nine months.

Define Your Reference Period

First, set an end date and a start date for your reference period. For the end of the reference period, use the last day of the most recently completed month or the last day of your company's regular performance evaluation period or budget year.

If you set the end of the period as March 31 and specify an analysis period of 12 months, then April 1 of the prior year is the start date of the reference period (and April 1 of this year begins the new period that you will use for your first forecast).

Record Reference Period Information

Once you've specified your reference period, answer the 10 questions about your activities during that period, as shown in the diagram included in this chapter. If this is your first time using systematic referral marketing, you probably can't answer all these questions. However, you will certainly be able to after you've completed your first new period.

The answers to the Reference Period Questions will establish a baseline against which you will measure your first forecast. A year from now (or after whatever period you specify), you can compare the results you realize from your referral marketing with the projections you are about to make.

Reference Period Questions

Start date: **4/01/2011**   End date: **3/31/2012**

Prospects
1. How many prospects did you generate or identify from all sources?   **50**
2. How many of these prospects were referred to you?   **30**
   What percentage of all prospects does this represent?   **60%**

Clients
3. How many new clients did you get from all sources?   **15**
4. How many of these new clients came from referrals?   **10**
   What percentage of all new clients does this represent?   **67%**

Sales
5. What was your sales total during the reference period?   **$150K**
6. How much of this was generated from referrals?   **$90K**
   What percentage of all sales does this represent?   **60%**

Referral Sources
7. How many sources provided the referred prospects
   identified in question 2?   **20**
8. What was the average number of referral prospects
   per source?   **2.5**
9. How many sources provided you with the new referred
   clients identified in question 4?   **6**
10. What was the average number of referred clients per source?   **2.5**

Your First Forecast

The next step is to write down what you expect to achieve during a future period. Your reference period determines your first forecast period. If your reference period is the year ending March 31, 2011, your forecast period is April 1, 2010–March 31, 2011.

To make your projections, you simply answer the same questions, slightly revised, by plugging in the appropriate data for the forecast period, then comparing your answers with the reference period. For example, you know that 30 prospects came to you by referral in the reference period (question 2 in the diagram), and you expect to get 45 new prospects by referral in your forecast period (question 2 in the First Period Projections diagram, also included in this chapter). This is a 50 percent increase $(15/30 = .50)$.

Your projections of total sales from this worksheet become part of your referral marketing plan. In our example, we expect total sales to be $200,000 (question 5 in the First Period Projections diagram), of which $150,000 — that is, 75 percent — will be from referrals (question 6 in the same diagram).

Sales Projections					
Product/ service	**Unit price**	**No. units expected to be sold**	**Total projected sales**	**Expected sales from referrals**	**Expected % sales from referrals**
Executive Coaching	$200/h	500	$100,000	$70,000	70%
CFO for Rent®	$5,000/ mo	10	$50,000	$35,000	70%
Exec. Search	$2,000	10	$20,000	$20,000	100%
Exec. Seminars	$3,000	10	$30,000	$25,000	83%
Tot. sales exp. during campaign period: A. $200,000 B. $150,000					
Expected % of total sales from referrals: C. 75 %					

In answering question 7 on the First Period Projection diagram, assume that the number of referrals generated by each source during period one will be the same as during the reference period. For example, if you averaged five referred prospects per source during the reference period, then you would need 100 sources (500 divided by 5) to get 500 referred prospects, or 1,400 (7,000 divided by 5) for 7,000 referred prospects.

First Period Projections

Start date: _**4/01/2011**_   End date: _**3/31/2012**_

Prospects

1. How many prospects do you expect to generate from all sources? | **60** |

   Forecast no. 1: The number of prospects generated will (increase/decrease) by | **+20** | % compared with the reference period.

2. How many of the prospects you generate do you expect to result from referrals? | **45** |

   What percentage of all prospects will this represent? | **75** % |

   Forecast no. 2: The percentage of prospects generated from referrals will (increase/decrease) by | **+50** % |

Clients

3. How many new clients do you expect to generate from all sources? | **20** |

   Forecast no. 3: The number of clients generated will (increase/decrease) by | **+33** | % compared with the reference period.

4. How many clients do you expect to generate from the referred prospects? | **15** |

   What percentage of all new clients will this represent? | **75** % |

   Forecast no. 4: The percentage of clients generated from referrals will (increase/decrease) by | **+50** % |

Sales

5. How much do you expect to generate in sales? $ | **200K** |

   Forecast no. 5: Total sales will (increase/decrease) by | **+33** | % compared with the reference period.

6. How much of the total sales do you expect to result from referred clients? $ | **150K** |

   What percentage of total sales will this represent? | **75** % |

   Forecast no. 6: Sales resulting from referrals will (increase/decrease) by $ | **+60K** |, and the percentage of total sales resulting from referrals will (increase/decrease) by | **+15** % |

Referral Sources

7. How many sources do you expect you will need to generate the expected number of referred prospects? | **30** |

   Forecast no. 7: The number of sources needed to generate the expected referred prospects will (increase/decrease) by | **+50** % |

8. What will be the average number of referred prospects per source? (Enter the reference period average.) | **2.5** |

9. How many sources do you expect will be needed to generate the number of referred clients you expect (using the average from reference period question 10)? | **6** |

10. What will be the average number of referred clients per source? (Enter the reference period average.) | **2.5** |

Beyond Period One

After you have completed one period of your referral marketing and com-pared the results with the projections based on your reference period, you'll be ready to adjust your referral marketing plan and set up new pro-jections. Close scrutiny of how your results diverged from your expecta-tions should help you forecast future results more accurately.

To forecast your referrals and sales for period two and beyond, simply make the previous period your new reference period, and then answer the questions as you did for your period one forecast.

This first step in determining desired outcome — projecting what you expect to achieve by the end of each period — gives your referral market-ing focus and direction. It also establishes several of the yardsticks that you will be using to evaluate its success.

⇒ *Action Item*

Enter your sales projections into the referral marketing plan you started in the previous chapter.

27

Tracking and Evaluating Results
Monitoring and Adjusting Your Plan

For an individual businessperson, as well as for an organization, an essential part of any marketing plan is measuring the results. Your referral marketing is no exception. To use your sources wisely and efficiently, you've got to know whether and how well your referral marketing is working, how you can change it to improve current and future results, and how much your investment of time and money is earning you.

Why Bother with Tracking??
(Answer: Because it *Pays* Well!)

Tracking where your business is coming from is crucial to working your referral marketing plan. Most business people that track referrals can tell you how much business they receive by referral. Where it starts to get a little fuzzy is when you ask who is giving those referrals and how the opportunities are presented. This is what we like to refer to as the part of the iceberg that is below the surface (see the Tip of the Iceberg diagram included in this chapter). The sales you can see include the customers in front of you, or revenue on your income statement. What doesn't show up are the beneath-the-surface activities, such as the referrals, speaking engagements, or your "giving activities."

The key to tracking the referral process lies in knowing what to measure. An effective referral marketing plan should be measured in three categories:

1. Networking activities
2. Referrals received
3. Closed business

When you do not track the referral process, the lag time between participating in networking activities, getting referrals, and ultimately closing

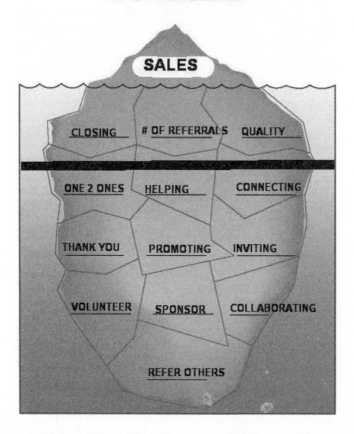

TIP OF THE ICEBERG

SALES

CLOSING   # OF REFERRALS   QUALITY

ONE 2 ONES   HELPING   CONNECTING

THANK YOU   PROMOTING   INVITING

VOLUNTEER   SPONSOR   COLLABORATING

REFER OTHERS

the resulting business inevitably creates a significant challenge. Without tracking the system, you cannot pinpoint which of your networking activities have led to the referrals that end up resulting in new business for you.

Now that you understand why tracking the referral process is important, let's look at some examples of networking activities and see how you can measure this first category in order to evaluate your referral process. Actions such as sending an article of interest or a thank you note, giving a referral, and meeting for lunch are all great examples of networking activities. To measure the effectiveness of these activities, you can use a tool called a Networking Scorecard (see the diagram included in this chapter). The Networking Scorecard allows you to plan your networking activities, track them, and then measure their effectiveness through a weekly point scale.

TIP #1 — In order to stay engaged in the process, reward yourself as you hit certain Networking Scorecard point benchmarks.

As you fill out your weekly Networking Scorecard, it is important to keep in mind that participation in networking activities does not often produce immediate results. In most cases these activities will take weeks, or even months, of lag time before they start producing referrals and closed business, which is precisely why it's important to track the process.

 REFERRAL® INSTITUTE

Networking Scorecard

Activity List	Available Points	4/21	4/22	4/23	4/24	4/25	4/26	4/27
NOTE CARDS & GIFTS:								
Send a notecard	2							
Send a gift	5							
Send an article of interest	5							
Submit a requested article for publication	20							
PHONE ACTIVITIES:								
Make a "How Are You" phone call to someone in your network	3							
MEETINGS WITH REFERRAL SOURCES/PARTNERS								
One to One – with someone in Visibility	5							
One to One - with someone in Credibility	10							
One to One - with someone in Profitability	15							
NETWORKING ACTIVITIES:								
# of people invited to a networking event (no points for spamming)	1							
# of people that attended networking event	5							
Execute any of the 18 Tactics to Motivate Referral Source	3							
Execute any of the 15 Ways to Promote Others	3							
SPEAKING ENGAGEMENTS:								
Arrange a speaking event for someone in your network	15							
REFERRAL ACTIVITIES								
I Bring my referral partner a closed deal	10							
I Describe products and services in person so well I can tell the person I am referring what the contact is looking for within their product or service	9							
I Qualify a prospects specific need or interest and arrange a 3-way face to face meeting where myself, the referral partner, and the prospect are all present	8							
I Qualify a prospects specific need or interest and connect the referral partner and the prospect (via email or phone) with the understanding they will meet for an appointment	7							
I Qualify a prospects specific need or interest and arrange permission for the referral partner to call the prospect	6							
I Send a letter of Introduction & Call	5							
I Send Letter of Recommendation with Testimonial	4							
I Authorize the Use of My Name	3							
I Give out Literature, Business card or Company Information	2							
I Give a Name and/or Contact Information Only	1							
COLLABORATIVE EVENT:								
# of people invited (no points for spamming)	1							
# of people invited that attended	5							
GRAND TOTALS		0	0	0	0	0	0	0

The second category that must be measured in the tracking process is the referrals that are received. Measuring this activity allows you to manage each referral and to follow up with the referred prospects, as well as with those who have referred you.

The final category to track is the closed business that results from your networking activities and the referrals that you receive. Along with tracking your results, you are able to tie back to who is referring you the business, and what activities have been most profitable in producing business. When you track your closed business, you will begin to see where your time is spent in order to produce the different results.

TIP #2 — Your biggest opportunity in tracking the referrals category is the ability to provide recognition to your Referral Sources and to ensure that you are not just a *taker* in the referral process.

But be forewarned: Though many people tend to slow down their networking activities when they start producing results and getting more business, this is a big mistake. Even though you may be receiving business, do not fall victim to a false sense of security, as you cannot disregard the lag time between participating in networking activities and closing business. Simply taking the time to implement a basic, easily carried out tracking system such as this can help you to realize a very successful referral process.

Victoria Trafton's experience in using this tracking system is one such success story. Victoria is a professional business trainer in Arizona, and she decided to begin scoring and tracking her weekly activities on a Networking Scorecard. Her first week began rather low, with only 82 points. Over the next several weeks, by deliberately planning activities and tracking them, she was able to move these points to 100 and then 200 points a week. At the same time, she was measuring the referrals she was receiving and, of course, she was ultimately able to measure the business that was closed from those referrals.

To evidence Victoria's success at tracking her referrals, let's look at what her monthly averages looked like after only six months of opening up her training business and implementing a referral process tracking system. Her networking activities were scoring over 200 points per week, she was giving 27 referrals a month on average, and receiving nine referrals plus three speaking engagements a month. As a result of her referrals, Victoria was closing over $11,000 in referred business for her training business a month!

TIP # 3 — Consistent tracking will provide you with an accurate return on networking investment, the value of a referred appointment and who your most profitable referral relationships are. Budgeting your time with the right activities and the right people is a major part of the art and science of networking.

Though this way of tracking your referral process is an excellent one, it is not the only way to track. One question that we are commonly asked is:

"OK, I get it, I need to track my referral process, but what do I track it with?"

Our answer to that question is:

WHATEVER METHOD YOU WILL ACTUALLY USE!

We have participants that are tracking their referral process on the networking scorecard above, others who have created their own spreadsheets, and still others using even more sophisticated tracking systems, such as Relate2Profit.

Try these tools for a while; if they don't fit, adapt them to suit your purposes. There are many different ways to track and evaluate the results of your referral marketing activities. Besides the logs, questionnaires, checklists, and profiles presented in this book, you can use computer software programs.

Remember: What you measure, you will attain!

Knowing Where You're Going

It's important to keep track of your results and to be as up to date as you can on how well your referral marketing is working. At first, you may feel that these tools take up too much of your valuable time. That's understandable. None of us enjoy all the paperwork it takes to maintain a business, especially information-reporting forms that seem to get sent off into limbo or stored away and forgotten. But if you get into the habit of keeping track of this information, and if you stay alert for and respond to changes, you'll find using these tools gets easier — and your increased business efficiency will more than make up for the time you spend.

With a thorough tracking and evaluation system, you'll know whether your plan is working and whether it's cost effective. You'll be able to demonstrate to managers, investors, bankers, and employees that you're a focused and capable marketing professional. Be patient, persistent, flexible, and imaginative, and you'll eventually find yourself running a successful referral-based business, one that will be the envy of other businesses.

⇒ *Action Items*

1. Track your previous week's giving activities.
2. Set a goal for next week's Networking Scorecard points.
3. Focus the majority of your time with people you are in Credibility and Profitability with. You can also be strategic by additionally focusing on Contact Spheres, Power Teams, and Referral Partners identified in Chapters 13 & 20.

28

Rewarding Referrals

Getting People to Send You Business

Creativity Works

You can greatly enhance your referral-based business by designing creative incentives for people to give you referrals. However, of all the key techniques for making the system work, this one seems to frustrate people the most.

Historically, finder's fees have been used as an incentive for giving someone referrals. Although finder's fees can be appropriate, we don't believe they are necessarily the best technique to employ in most situations. Here is an excellent example from Ivan of a nonmonetary incentive system:

Years ago I went to my chiropractor for a routine adjustment. Several weeks before, I had referred a friend to him who had recently been in an accident. As I walked into the waiting room, I noticed a bulletin board that was displayed prominently on the wall. The bulletin board read, "We would like to thank the following patients for referring someone to us last month."

Actually, there was nothing unusual about this sign. It had been there on each of my previous visits, except this time my name was posted on it. I took notice and was pleased, but didn't give it a second thought until a month later, when I returned and saw that my name was no longer on it. Instantly I thought: Who else can I refer to the doctor so that my name will be put back on the board? For the record, I did come up with another referral for the good doctor.

Something like this may not work for everyone. But if it worked on me, I'm sure it will have a positive effect on others. The key is to select several incentive options so as to impact as many people as possible.

The Importance of Incentives

An incentive in this context is anything that gets people to refer you to others. Many doctors' offices use the same technique as the chiropractor in Ivan's story. It works well for at least two reasons:

1. The bulletin board is a continual reminder to patients that the office wants their referrals.
2. People like to be recognized for their efforts.

Some health care professionals offer a free visit when a referral becomes a new patient. Other business professionals send small gift baskets, bottles of wine, flowers, or certificates for their services or the services of other businesses in the community. Depending on the type of product or service you offer and the relationship with your referring parties, you may also employ:

- Free estimates, samples, or analyses
- Additional products or services for no extra cost
- Product or service discounts
- Product or service time extensions
- Extended telephone consultation privileges
- Extended or life memberships
- Exclusive or charter memberships
- Group discounts
- Extended warranties
- Reduced costs on peripheral items or services

One enterprising entrepreneur developed a program whereby an existing customer would receive a $500 bonus coupon toward a purchase on his next order for referring a new customer. In this case, each new customer represented several thousands of dollars worth of business, so the $500 bonus coupon was a bargain.

When you offer any type of discount or novelty item as an incentive for referrals, keep in mind what your cost would be to generate a new client or customer from scratch, including the cost of printed literature, advertisements, sales calls, telephone time, meetings, appointments, and so forth. You can readily see that the cost of gaining a new client through a referral incentive program is almost always lower.

Incentive programs also help you sell more products or services more frequently to your existing customer base. Again, these are sales that are generated at a far lower marketing cost and effort.

Incentive Triangulation

Some resourceful business people use a technique that we call "Incentive Triangulation." This is a powerful way of leveraging other people's services to benefit your customers, clients, or patients. The concept is simple and can be designed to fit the needs or requirements of any business. For example, a retailer might negotiate an arrangement with another local business, such as a florist, printer, or appliance storeowner, whereby that store will provide their customers with a discount of 10 percent or more on their next purchase. Thereafter, each time someone gives you a referral, reward him or her with whatever you would normally give as an incentive and also a coupon good for the discount at the prearranged business.

Incentive Triangulation

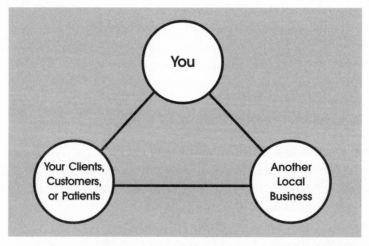

This form of joint venture is beneficial for all three parties, hence the term "Incentive Triangulation." You benefit because you are providing another incentive for people to refer you. The other business benefits because you are sending your clients to it, along with a recommendation, of course. Finally, your clients benefit because they get recognition for their effort as well as an additional product or service at a reduced rate. Granted, this type of incentive may not be appropriate for all professions. Where appropriate, however, it works very well.

Finding the Right Incentive Program

No matter what form of incentive program you use, the fact that you offer incentives means that your potential for generating business by referral will increase. The question is, What type of incentive will work for *you*?

To meet the challenge of finding the right incentive program, tap into the assistance and insights of other people. An effective way to do this is to invite about 10 people you know to meet with you. Include a representative sample of your customers/clients/patients, business associates, partners, and friends. Their purpose is to think up incentives you could offer to produce a larger referral-based business. Host a lunch or dinner for the group and either take copious notes or tape-record the meeting. Invite those who are willing to donate about two hours for your benefit (and receive a free meal, of course).

Prepare yourself well in advance of the group meeting. Think the subject over beforehand so you have an idea of the limits that you may need to set for an incentive program, such as cost, duration, appropriateness, etc. Make sure to provide some notepads, a preliminary questionnaire, sample materials, a flip chart, and even a few ideas to get the ball rolling. If you're going to discuss a product, bring actual samples to give the group a point of reference.

Begin the actual session by clearly stating a specific problem. Make sure your group understands that the incentive has to be geared to the group you've targeted. Explain that you are looking for a variety of ideas and that you won't make any immediate decisions.

Brainstorming

The concept of brainstorming was originated by Alex F. Osborn to help trigger creative ideas in advertising. Following the meal, you or a designated party leads a brainstorming session to generate ideas on an effective incentive program for your business. For maximum creativity, four basic principles must be fully understood and followed, according to Osborn:

1. **Judicial judgment is ruled out.** Criticism of ideas must be withheld until later; otherwise, you run the risk of shutting down the idea pipeline. The first time we used brainstorming, we tried to evaluate each idea as it came up, and the entire session went way too long.
2. **"Freewheeling" is welcome.** The wilder the idea, the better; it's easier to tame down ideas than to think them up. Moreover, wild ideas often lead to creative solutions. We've found that the way an idea is first presented by someone doesn't always register with others. With a twist and turn, however, ideas seemingly from Mars are brought back to Earth and become eminently workable.
3. **Quantity is desirable.** The greater the number of ideas, the better the likelihood of winners. Don't be afraid if you have to go to the second or third page of a flip chart. You want at least 12 ideas so you'll have plenty to work with once everyone runs out of steam.
4. **Combination and improvement are also desirable.** In addition to contributing ideas of their own, participants should suggest how ideas of others can be turned into better ideas, or how two or more ideas can be joined into still another idea. Some ideas that aren't workable alone become quite effective in combination.

Once you've exhausted all the ideas for possible incentives, review the list item by item and try to narrow it down to a manageable number. Don't worry about how you're going to do something until you've determined all the options. After most of the ideas are exhausted, spend time discussing those that are left and get feedback on which ones may be most effective. Last, select the idea or ideas that you'll put into practice.

The process we've just reviewed is known as the "focus-group technique." Such groups have been used in market research for many years and are excellent for gathering data as well as probing attitudes on many marketing-related subjects.

At the end of the session, if the sparks were really flying, suggest that the group meet again soon. As such, it could evolve from a one- or two-time focus group into your own advisory board. Even if you meet quarterly or semiannually, there is still great value in having reconvened to discuss the challenges you're working on.

Creative Incentives

Creativity is the key to any good incentive program. People just naturally like to help each other, but especially when they know their efforts are successful. Let your contact know when a referral he or she has made comes through, and be as creative as you can.

We've heard many novel ways business people reward those who send them referrals. A female consultant sends bouquets of flowers to men. An owner of a music store sends concert tickets. A financial planner sends change purses and money clips.

An accountant in St. Louis thanks those who successfully refer a client to him by paying for a dinner for two at an exclusive restaurant at least one hour's drive from their homes. This approach firmly plants the accountant in the minds of his Referral Sources: They won't be able to use it right away because the distance requires that they plan for it. And as the date approaches, because it has been planned, they'll be talking about it and probably about the accountant. Later, when the referring party runs into someone else who might need an accountant, which one do you think he will recommend? Here's a great story by Ivan to illustrate this point:

One realtor I met in Northern California told me that for almost six years he had offered a one-hundred-dollar finder's fee to anyone giving him a referral that led to a listing or sale. He said that in all that time he had given only about a dozen finder's fees, so he decided to try another kind of incentive.

Living on a large parcel of land in prime wine country, he had begun growing grapes in his own vineyard. A thought occurred to him: Why not take the next step? He began processing the grapes and bottling his own special vintage wine. After his first harvest, he had a graphic artist design a beautiful label, which he affixed to each bottle. He told all his friends that he did not sell this wine; he gave it as a gift to anyone providing him with a bona fide referral.

He gave away dozens of cases in the first three years — half the time it took him to give only one dozen cash finder's fees. Yet each bottle cost him less than 10 dollars to produce. This special vintage wine makes him infinitely more money than giving away a handful of hundred-dollar finder's fees.

About two weeks after the first edition of this book went to the printer, I got a call from the Realtor. "Has your book gone into print?" he asked. I told him it had. "Too bad," he replied. "I've got a terrific story for you.

"Last Friday I got a phone call from a woman I didn't know. Out of the blue, she gave me two referrals. As I wrote down the information, I asked her how she had heard of me.

"She said, 'I had dinner last night at a friend's house. He served wine. I took a sip. "Wow, great wine!" I told him. "Where did you buy it?" "You can't buy it," he said. "The only way you can get it is to give this real estate agent a referral."

"'I have two referrals,' she said. 'Can I get two bottles?'

"So I gladly sent her two bottles. Both referrals turned into business, and each of them cost me only 10 dollars."

It sometimes amazes us, even now, how something as simple as a bottle of wine can be such a powerful incentive for people to give you referrals. But the explanation is really quite simple: because it's special. A bottle of wine that can't be bought can be worth 10 times what it cost to produce when traded for something as valuable as a business referral.

Incentives for Those Around You

Are there employees, co-workers, friends, or relatives who might be able to refer you? It always surprises us that people forget to provide incentives for the individuals working with them. You'll probably need to offer different kinds of incentives for different groups of people. You may choose to offer something completely different for your employees than you would for your clients or networking associates, such as bonuses and vacation days.

Remember, most individuals who are preparing to score big by building business by referral consider finding the right incentive to be their biggest challenge. If this is you, make it easier on yourself: be sure to get opinions and feedback from others who have a significant interest in your success.

Don't underestimate the value of recognizing the people who send you business. A well-thought-out incentive program will add much to your referral marketing program.

⇛ *Action Items*

1. Commit to a system that recognizes every referral you receive, whether it turns into business or not.
2. Find a personal way to recognize each referral. The documented GAINS profile on your Referral Source is one place to find this information. You may also want to ask someone that may know them well.
3. Lead your focus group in a brainstorming session to generate ideas for an effective incentive program for your business. Avoid criticizing any ideas, welcome freewheeling, seek many ideas, and piggyback on the ideas presented.
4. Identify the businesses in your market that can help you implement the Incentive Triangulation strategy.

29

Attracting Hot Referrals

The Keys to Getting Good Referrals

Begin by Asking for Them

It always amazes us, when we speak with business professionals looking for referrals, to find out that they haven't really asked their friends, associates, networking partners, customers, clients, or patients for a referral. Mind you, most people will initially say they've asked for referrals, but when we've probed, we found that quite often they asked for referrals from a very small percentage of their contacts and, having not received a favorable response, they've pretty much dropped the effort.

A very effective approach for asking someone for a referral is outlined in a book called *Referrals*, which was written by Mark Sheer (whom we first introduced in Chapter 9). In his book, Mark strongly recommends that the phrase you need to use when asking for a referral is, "I'm expanding my business and I need your help. Who do you know who . . . ?" Mark goes on to say:

> You must NOT alter this phrase. It has been tried and proven successful. Other phrases have been tried and have not produced the desired results — so don't waste your time using them. Once you become comfortable with this new phrase, it is very easy to ask your contact for a referral by simply saying, "Who do you know who . . .?"

This approach provides you with an open-ended question format that allows people to think about the ways they may be able to refer to you. Most people who do not get a positive response to their request for referrals fail because they have asked a very specific, closed-ended question such as, "Do you know anyone who needs my service?"

Ironically, while we were writing the material for this chapter, Ivan received a letter from a woman from whom he had purchased some children's educational toys over the years. She had obviously taken one of Mark's seminars, because I received the following letter (italics mine):

Dear Dr. Misner:

Just a note to thank you for your business and support. I am expanding my business and I need your help. *Who do you know who* matches my ideal customer profile? I would be thrilled if you would take a few minutes to make a list of acquaintances and friends who could benefit from my services; people and companies you believe want or need the quality service and follow-up I will provide. Please read and fill out the enclosed "Customer Profile." I will give you a call by the end of the week. In the meantime, please feel free to send in the profile using the enclosed self-addressed stamped envelope. Thank you in advance.

Who do you know who is having a baby?

Who do you know who is a new parent, grandparent, aunt or uncle?

Who do you know who needs developmental toys for their children?

Who do you know who belongs to an organization or group that donates to children's groups, such as Toys for Tots, Pediatric AIDS Foundation, etc.?

Who do you know who is a teacher?

Who do you know who wants a career that directly affects the future of the world through the education of children?

Sincerely,

S.L.

Educational Toys Consultant

By listing people he knows who fit the description she outlined above, Ivan is giving her tacit approval to use his name when she contacts them. The only thing better than this would be for him to say something to them himself.

Just Ask, Right? (No.)

You now understand the power of asking for referrals, but before we go on, we want to remind you of the VCP Process® we discussed earlier in this book. Here's a story from Mike:

> *I recently attended a BNI National Conference, and there was a lot of effective networking going on. With the culture of Givers Gain®, there were participants offering to help one another and make connections. However, on several occasions, I also saw some business people walk up to others who barely knew them and ask to be referred to one or more valued relationships. I felt awkward whenever I heard these conversations.*
>
> *I think what I was actually feeling was déjà vu. I've been on the receiving end of the "referral ambush" before, when people I was hardly in the Visibility phase with have asked me to expose my reputation by referring them to one of my valued relationships. In some cases, I was even asked to promote them or their companies to my entire database!*
>
> *During this particular Conference, there was one participant who approached the keynote speaker and introduced herself. Shortly into the conversations, she let the speaker know that she understood the speaker knew an internationally known personality, and that she would like an introduction to that person in order to pitch her business to him. WOW . . . that was a big ask.*
>
> *So, why did it feel inappropriate? Part of the reason is the stage of the referral process, or the VCP Process®, that the attendee and speaker were engaged in.*
>
> *In the Visibility stage, two people simply know who each other are.*
>
> *In fact, in this situation, the attendee was actually in the pre-Visibility stage with the speaker. It's true that the attendee might have mistakenly felt that she was in the Credibility phase with the speaker, maybe felt that she knew him, since she had been watching him connect with the audience repeatedly over the course of the three-day event. However, it's important to always remember that Credibility is something that is established over a substantial period of time — not in just a few hours, days, or weeks. It takes months, and in many cases years, to develop real credibility with someone.*

To clarify, I do believe that in order to get referrals we need to ask. The key, however, is to know how to ask and when it is appropriate to make the request. When is the right time, you may ask? The right time to ask for a referral is when both parties are in the Credibility phase of the referral relationship.

*Networking should not be a system that ends up alienating your friends and family. Be conscious of the deposits you make into your relationships before you start "writing checks" or, in essence, **asking for referrals** from those with whom you have relationships.*

The Value of Testimonials

An important part of having a positive message delivered effectively is knowing how to cultivate relationships in such a way as to have others talking about you positively. Having someone tell a group of people how good your product or service is beats anything you can say about yourself. This is called a "testimonial."

Proactively seeking and giving testimonials should be as deliberate as seeking and giving referrals in your marketing plan. Too many times we see outstanding business people have wonderful things said about them and do nothing with it. In some cases, a testimonial can be more valuable than a referral. Think about it — When you have a well-formed testimonial from a credible person, that becomes a recyclable recommendation. You can now ask them to post it on your LinkedIn account, include it on your website, brochures, and other marketing material. You should also provide these testimonials to your Referral Sources so they can appropriately use them when they are referring you.

When we are giving presentations, we often use testimonials to demonstrate how others have used the principles we're discussing and the results they received. The testimonial used properly is also a powerful sales tool. Let's say you're talking with a prospect that is a financial planner, and they're evaluating whether investing in training will give them a good return on investment. What better time to present a testimonial of another financial planner that invested in the training and communicate the results they received.

Getting and giving good testimonials should be proactive and thought out. When people you know have experienced your products or services ask them about it:

1. What was it like before they used your products or service?
2. What was their experience like when they used your products or services?
3. What were the benefits of working with you?

Rather than just ask for testimonials, make it easy for them by reforming their comments in the format illustrated above. Once you have written it out for them, ask them if it accurately describes their experience and if you could have their permission to use it. You should also take advantage of the opportunity to promote them by identifying them by name, company, website, contact information, logo, and photo.

We've included in this chapter a testimonial given for Phil Bedford, the Referral Institute Master Franchisee for the Middle East.

Hi Phil — I know this has been a long time coming, but I do not give testimonials for the sake of it, only when I have witnessed great service or benefit.

I am now into week 10 of the Referral Institute Certified Networker® Programme, and am delighted with the results so far. I can categorize my ROI in three areas, as stated below:

1. Financially — I received business to twice the value of my initial investment in the programme, within four weeks.
2. Personally — I am 46 years of age, and quite honestly thought of myself as a good networker, therefore somewhat skeptical of the possible benefits of the programme. I also almost convinced myself that I really did not have time to commit to the programme for the full 12 weeks. How wrong I was! I now have a full kit of referral tools that I can use with ease and confidence, giving me absolute certainty that 95% of my future business will come from referral marketing.
3. My referral partners — I have already generated in excess of AED 700,000 for my referral partners via other members of the Certified Networker® programme — the caliber of the delegates is so high that I am convinced that number will grow and grow.

I could not recommend the programme more highly for anybody who actually wants to learn how to achieve real success in referral marketing, as long as you are willing to adopt all that is taught.

I wish you every success with the programme, Phil Bedford. I will certainly re-enroll on an annual basis to ensure I keep the learning fresh!

Best Regards

Peter Cowan

Realtime Learning, Dubai

Giving testimonials to your Referral Sources is also a valuable way to invest in the relationship. Dawn Lyons and Eddie Esposito, both Vice Presidents of the Referral Institute, add recommendations into their email signatures to promote their key contacts.

We've included a sample of Dawn's email signature in this chapter.

Email Signature Sample — Dawn Lyons

Dawn Lyons

As a referral organization, we highly recommend . . .

Zach Mesel, Computer Networking Expert with Wooden Spoon Technologies, Inc.

Zach uses his 20+ years of industry experience to help business owners keep their computer networks up and their support costs down. If you know business owners in Santa Rosa who have networks of at least 20 computers, Zach can do a consultation with them about how to make their support and budget processes hassle-free.

PLUS, if you didn't know this, Zach was selected to host all of the Referral Institute's websites worldwide!! We are very proud to have Zach and his company on our team!

I recall visiting a BNI chapter and watching one of the members who knew the value of testimonials, particularly how to *give* testimonials. Rather than just stand up and tell everyone how great Jane was, or verbally talk about his experience, he took the time to write up a well-drafted testimonial on his letterhead that he read and presented to

Jane. In addition to this, he created a testimonial binder, which was left for the visitors to see when they signed in. WOW!! This made an impression on Jane and everyone else in the room.

—MIKE MACEDONIO

Many years ago, a chiropractor who was a member of BNI asked me what he could do to start getting some business from his chapter. I asked him if anyone in the chapter had ever used his services. He said, no. I asked him if anyone in the group had ever used any chiropractor. He said, probably not.

I told him that the best way for him to get some business was to get at least one member to use his services. Chiropractic care, like any form of health care, is personal. I suggested that he offer a special members-only discount that would persuade at least one member to use his services.

At the next meeting, he announced that he would take insurance as payment in full. Thus, anyone covered by a major medical plan would pay nothing to use him. Only one person took him up on this generous offer. The chiropractor was disappointed.

At the following meeting, the member who had recently used his services stood up and addressed the group: "I went to our chiropractor this week, and all I can say is that I have been an IDIOT! I can't believe that I've waited all these years to go see a chiropractor. This guy is GREAT! You're all CRAZY if you don't take him up on his offer. I've always had this little back problem. I didn't think it was any big deal, but I didn't know how much this thing was bothering me until it wasn't there any more. I FEEL GREAT!"

When he sat down, another member joked, "What the heck, he's still walking, I guess I'll try it too." The following week, this member came to the meeting and gave the chiropractor a good referral for another client. In short, the chiropractor received four new clients in a couple of weeks, all because someone stood up and said, "I've used his services and you should, too, *because.* . . ."

I've highlighted the word "because" so you will understand that an effective testimonial is good only if someone is specific about the person's service or product and provides details as to *why* it was good and how it helped. Such testimonials become shared experiences with the

others present, thus putting everyone much more at ease about the
service or product being offered.

— IVAN MISNER

Ask people who have used your products or services to talk to others
about their experience. In addition, whenever possible, have them give
you a testimonial letter you can use when speaking to people they know.

It's important as well for you to give testimonials about the people and
the businesses you've used. In their book *Putting the One-Minute Manager
to Work*, Ken Blanchard and Robert Lorber say that feedback on performance is one of the most crucial elements in dealing effectively with people. They suggest that feedback reinforces continued good performance.
When you have a chance to give a testimonial, you should talk about the
services or products you've used, and be specific about how it worked out.
In a meeting environment, simply giving everyone a laundry list of the
products you've used doesn't help anyone.

If you're active in various business networking groups, especially
strong contact networks, you'll find that testimonials are an integral element of the process. It's important not only to receive them, but to give
them as well. Testimonials add credibility and trust to those with whom
you are trying to build a referral-based business. In addition to testimonials, however, there are other things you should consider in making sure
you get your fair share of referrals.

Support Material and Techniques

Below are some effective ways to influence people to refer you. Some of
these may not work for everyone. The idea is to select those you think you
can apply in your own business or profession.

Samples. If you have an opportunity to distribute your materials, do
it. Bring products, samples, brochures, or a presentation book. Many networking groups provide a brochure table where you can place these items.
If people can see, feel, touch, hear, or smell samples of the product or service you provide, they are more likely to use you. Offer special, members-
only prices or services. If you can get network members to use you, then,
like the chiropractor, they are much more likely to refer you.

Presentation books. Everyone active in networking groups can benefit by developing a presentation book. Buy a high-quality, three-ring binder that can attractively display samples of your products or services, brochures, photographs, etc. Take this to your meetings and make sure it gets circulated.

Free presentations or demonstrations. Many business professionals offer to speak free of charge to service clubs or business organizations as a way of getting exposure and promoting their business. If your product or service is conducive to this approach, tell the members of your personal network that you offer this service, and accept speaking engagements as bona fide referrals. Ask them to pitch you to the program chairs of organizations to which they belong.

If you're well prepared and do a good job at these presentations, you may find yourself getting many more speaking offers and a lot of new business. This technique is effective for almost any profession, but it's particularly helpful for consultants, therapists, financial planners, CPAs, and attorneys.

Door prizes. Smart business professionals know that people who have tried their products or services will probably use them again. We highly recommend that you offer door prizes regularly at your networking groups and ensure that you are given credit for the door prize when it is given. Always attach a business card so the winner knows where to get more.

Keep in touch regularly. Meet people outside of the normal meetings that you go to whenever you can. Write cards or letters, send articles that might be of interest, call to check in, let them know about a local business mixer, have lunch, play racquetball, tennis, or golf. Reinforce the relationship with a thank-you note. If someone gives you a referral or important information, send a thank-you note or gift basket. This reinforcement will strengthen the bond and encourage that person to think of you again.

Follow-Up. Knowing how to get referrals is really a matter of knowing how to be helpful to the people you associate with and how to ask for help in return. A successful referral marketing program involves creating an effective support system for yourself that also works to the advantage of others.

All the networking in the world, however, serves no purpose if you don't follow up effectively with the people you meet or who are referred to you. We've seen people who work hard at making contacts, but whose follow-up was so bad that the contacts were lost. It's as if they networked halfway, and then completely lost sight of the potential to generate business by referral. Follow-up letters and phone calls set the stage for further contact. All things being equal, the more you're in contact with others, the more business you'll generate. Today, more than ever, there's no excuse for not following up. Why? Because there are many companies on the market that produce numerous follow-up cards, thank-you cards, and contact cards especially designed for networking.

Schedule "reconnection calls" regularly. Such calls enable you to remind the new contacts who you are, where you met them, and what you do, as well as help you stay in touch with your long-term contacts. If you don't follow up with a phone call or letter, you will surely lose many business opportunities.

Unexpected Referral Sources

Sometimes good referrals come from sources that you least expect. Many business people we meet want to network exclusively with CEOs and corporate presidents. They tell us they don't want to join most business groups because top executives aren't members. If you're waiting to find a group exclusively for CEOs and top managers, don't hold your breath.

Even when you find such a group, it probably won't help. You see, they don't want you! They're hiding from you. Top business executives insulate themselves from those they think might try to sell them products or services. However, if you develop a referral-based business, there's no problem. You can increase your volume of business through referrals because you know a hundred people, who know a hundred people, who in turn know a hundred people, and so on. You are potentially linked to a vast network beyond your own, and you never know who may be in this extended network.

The owner of a drapery business told me about one referral he received. A friend referred an elderly woman to him because the friend thought that he could help her. The woman, who was in her late seventies, had sought the help of many drapery companies, to no avail. She wanted to install a pull blind on a small window in the back door of her home. She feared that people going by could look in. The woman explained that normally her son would take care of this, but he was on an extended business trip. No area drapery company would help her because it would be expensive to come out and install a small blind like that. The businessman agreed to help her because a mutual friend referred her to him, and because she was obviously worried about the situation.

About a month later, the businessman was working in his warehouse/showroom when he noticed an expensive stretch limo pull up in front of his commercial building. Curious, he watched as the chauffeur got out and opened the door for a man dressed in an expensive suit.

The man came into the businessman's showroom and asked for the proprietor. The businessman introduced himself and asked how he could help the gentleman. The man asked whether he remembered the elderly woman for whom he had installed the small blind. The businessman said he remembered her well. The man said that he was impressed that the businessman did this job, because he knew that there was no money in it.

The woman, he said, was his mother, and she had raved about how nice the businessman was and how he had helped her when no one else would. She had instructed her son to use the businessman's service whenever he could. The son told him that he had a new, 6,000-square-foot home by the ocean. He asked the businessman to go out and take measurements because he wanted to install window coverings throughout the entire house.

The businessman told me that it was the most profitable job he had ever received, and it came from a little old woman who needed a small blind on her back door.

Ironically, the "great referral" you receive is probably not going to come from a CEO, but from someone who *knows* a CEO.

An architect in Las Vegas told me about a window washer he met in one of his networking groups. He said he saw the window washer every week for over nine months before the window washer gave him his first referral. This one referral, however, was worth over $300,000 to the architect!

— DR. IVAN MISNER

You never know where a good referral may come from. It may come from a little old lady or a cab driver or a window washer, as mentioned in Ivan's story in this chapter. So don't ignore the possibilities of the contacts that other business people have or can make for you.

What If You Get a Bad Referral?

You got a "BAD" referral, so what should you do?

How about starting with, "Thank You?"

The fact that someone was thinking about and took action has to be a good start. The next thing you can do is define what a "BAD" referral is. Too many times when we have the conversation with business people about the quality of their referrals we are surprised at what they qualify as a bad referral. Does the fact that they didn't do business qualify as a bad referral? What if the referred prospect needs what you have, is interested to find out more, but then realizes it's outside their budget? Remember, we have defined (in Chapter 2) a referral as *a recommendation of a person or business to someone who has a need for your products or services and is willing to connect.* It would be unrealistic to expect that every referral is guaranteed business or else it would be a bad referral.

What are your qualifiers for a bad referral?

1. Getting referred for something you don't do or to an area you don't cover? This would be a clear example of a referral that doesn't fit your business. At the same time, what about the opportunity for you to be able to referral them to someone that can help them? You have just been given a great chance to make a contribution to the relationship of the non-qualified prospect referred to you and the person you refer that can help them.

2. Being referred to people you don't want to do business with? Can you define clearly what you want and don't want? How many times have you heard business people say I'm looking for "anybody who . . ."? Really? How about people who don't pay? Or people who are always unsatisfied? For us a "bad" referral would be a business owner with a bad attitude, indifferent about their business, someone who should have never gotten in business and won't be in business much longer.

3. Is there a minimum level of introduction that you would act on? For example, would you act on just having a person's contact information, or only if the person has a need for your service and has agreed to take your call?

> Whatever standard you put in place for a good or bad referral, the responsibility to educate your Referral Sources will be yours.

Whatever standard you put in place for a good or bad referral, the responsibility to educate your Referral Sources will be yours. When you do receive the "bad" referral, this is your opportunity to further train your Referral Source. Ignoring the referral will have you leaving money on the table. Why not go to the Referral Source and discuss what can be done differently to make it an effective introduction? If the referral is very weak, maybe they would be willing to make a personal introduction and give a testimonial. If they can't or won't, you can always let them know that you will not be acting on the referral right now.

The best way to avoid bad referrals is to tell people when they've given you one. Tell them tactfully, but tell them! If you don't, you'll keep getting bad referrals, and you'll deserve every one of them. We continually run into people who say, "Oh, I can't tell someone that the referral was no good." We say, "You can't afford not to tell him." Be direct, and don't apologize. They need to know the referral was bad.

Be positive, and make sure they know it was the referral they gave that was bad, and not their effort. If you expect the best from people, you'll usually get it. If you expect less than the best, you'll usually get that, too. The best way to ensure that you don't get bad referrals is to teach people what you consider to be a good referral. This differs for each person, and especially for each profession.

For example, some professionals, such as consultants, counselors, and therapists, consider the opportunity to give a speech to a business group a good referral. Others, such as printers, contractors, or florists, normally don't. You cannot assume that everyone knows what kind of referral you're seeking. You need to be very specific about what constitutes a good referral for you.

⇒ Action Items

1. Approach the last two clients that praised your work and ask them for permission to document their comments in the form of a testimonial. Help them by drafting the testimonial. Publish the testimonial only after you get their permission and approval. The testimonial should also promote them by having their name, company information, logo, or a headshot.

2. Draft two testimonials for your two best Contact Sphere relationships. Present it to them with an offer that if there is any wording
   that they would like changed, you would be happy to do it.
3. Create a list of people you will be asking for referrals. Keep in
   mind that when in the VCP Process®, it is appropriate to ask.
4. Script out what your specific referral request is.

30

The Last Part of the Secret

This chapter is for those of you who are now fully invested in referral marketing, yet may be a bit frustrated because you are not seeing the results you want, even after carefully putting in place what you've learned in the previous chapters of this book.

The 3 Core Competencies

In referral marketing the process of receiving successful referrals relies on three "core competencies":

1. You must receive the right referral marketing knowledge.
2. You have to stay engaged and immersed in the information.
3. You have to get your referral network trained by experts.

Let's look at these core competencies individually and see why they are so important.

1. **Gaining the right referral marketing knowledge:**
   This is crucial to your success! Most people did not take college courses on referral marketing, nor did they receive any referral marketing training when they opened up their business, yet they are all searching for more referrals! Ask yourself this question: How much have you invested into your referral marketing education? Do you have the right education on how to get out there and do it effectively? If not, then you may want to do some research on referral marketing! Ivan has written several books on the art of gaining business by referral, including the *New York Times* best-seller, *Truth or Delusion: Busting Networking's Biggest Myths*. It will

show you the right ways to be out there networking your business and building your Referral Sources!

2. **Staying engaged and immersed in this new information is an absolute must!**

   Many of us have taken a training program and can easily get excited about what we learned, think it was the best training ever, and even change a few things in our business — but if we forget to implement it on a regular basis, what happens? We simply go back to our old habits. Our old habits probably are not going to get us to our goals, so how do we stay engaged?

   You have to become part of a community of people who are also using the information on a regular basis. If you do, you have a much higher likelihood of using the information on a consistent basis. This is what will bring you to a higher level of success! The Referral Institute offers the *"Referrals For Life®"* program, which brings you the opportunity to be involved in a one-year program where you can attend any and all of the training programs offered in your area, plus all of the other members of the *"Referrals For Life® Community"* will help you stay on track and utilize the knowledge more consistently.

3. **Getting your referral network trained by experts:**

   The third competency is one that is often overlooked by those less experienced in building a business by referral. However, we cannot stress enough the importance of training your referral network. You may be a networking "superstar," but if you have a network of amateurs in referral networking, you will get amateur results.

This is what almost every system misses in the referral marketing process. Think about this — you have gained new knowledge about referral marketing by reading and implementing the skills you have learned in this book. You might have even taken the additional step of working with the Referral Institute and staying engaged by getting involved in a local *"Referrals For Life®"* program.

> You may be a networking "superstar," but if you have a network of amateurs in referral networking, you will get amateur results.

Now you have *almost* everything you need. However, you are still reliant upon other people giving you referrals. You have all the knowledge, you stay engaged in the information, but the people referring you don't have the same level of knowledge!

They will only be able to refer you based on their own skill level. The key is getting your Referral Sources trained to the same level. You can take the time and attempt to do it yourself, or you can bring them to many of the learning opportunities provided by Referral Institute.

The Referral Institute's senior management team experienced a significant turning point a few years ago when they realized this very important point, and they created a program module that literally *trained* the people in their clients' networks, for the client.

We urge you not to forget the third core competency as you develop your referral marketing plan. You need to ask yourself some questions, and answer them honestly:

1. Are your key Referral Sources knowledgeable and skillful with referral marketing?
2. At the most basic level, do they know who you are, what you do, and who your targeted prospects are?
3. Since referral marketing is a team approach, wouldn't it help if those in your network were also knowledgeable and skillful with referral generation?

You'll be amazed at how much more effective your referral relationship will be when your referral partner has a complete referral marketing plan *and* you're part of it. Now not only do they know who and how to refer you, but they now know *why* they should be referring you. It is part of their plan. To use a sports analogy, it starts by making sure we are playing the same sport. From there we want to be running plays from the same playbook. With execution and practice, we become a cohesive and productive scoring team. As Referral Institute Vice President Dawn Lyons has stated many times: "Referral marketing — you just can't do it alone."

Conclusion

The fact that you have read this book is evidence of your commitment to referral marketing knowledge. We hope that you will continue in your pursuit to gain new knowledge on referral marketing, and that you will stay engaged with consistent execution of your referral marketing plan. With this continued effort, you will be living the first two core competencies for referral success: Getting educated on referral marketing and staying immersed and engaged in the material.

Do remember, though, that the third core competency is the crucial one for you to achieve the level of success that you deserve: Having a referral team that is as educated and skilled in networking at the same level as you. You can educate yourself to a genius level and master the skills of referral marketing, yet still be disappointed with your results if you have surrounded yourself with an inadequate referral team.

It has been our intention with this book to give you the information to create your referral marketing plan. We also encourage you to stay immersed and engaged with the material. Finally, we hope that you will build a high quality referral team with knowledgeable, devoted professionals.

Glossary

Contact Sphere A contact sphere is a group of businesses or professions that complement, rather than compete with, your business.

Hub Firm A hub firm is the key business in a constellation of independent businesses tethered to one another to make the most effective use of the organizational strengths of each. Cooperative relationships between these businesses can be the source of dramatic competitive strength. Generally, the cooperative firms have a Contact Sphere (or symbiotic) relationship, as we described earlier. The difference here, however, is that one of the companies of this Contact Sphere, ideally yours, is the organizer or "hub" of the inter-related parties.

A hub firm network generally applies to consulting professions where multiple areas of expertise — or other resources that your company cannot supply directly — is required. It will allow you to operate at a higher level and provide greater service than you can alone.

In many cases, this hub firm network may be unlikely to reciprocate referrals on a regular basis. Reciprocal referrals are not the primary purpose of the organizer. Being able to provide more specialized services, operating further up the food chain and creating a competitive advantage are the motives. The hub firm organizer will have this network representing their support network more than their referral network.

Marketing buzz, or just "buzz," This is a term used in word-of-mouth marketing. The interaction of consumers and users of a product or service serve to amplify the original marketing message. This is also sometimes used in conjunction with Viral Marketing.

Memory Hook A memory hook is something in your presentation that so vividly describes what you do, that a person will be able to visualize it clearly in her mind's eye. This visualization of your product or service makes it easier for people to remember you whenever they meet someone who needs your service.

A memory hook would be appropriately used with a group of people you don't know at all, or who may be in the early stages of the VCP Process®.

Networking Networking is the process of developing and using contacts to increase your business, enhance your knowledge, expand your sphere of influence, or serve the community.

To be successful with business networking, you should understand that networking is about helping others as a way of growing your business. By helping others, they would be willing to help you or connect you to people they know.

Network Marketing This term is often used in multi-level marketing organizations to describe their marketing system. This type of marketing would have distributors sign up other distributors to sell their products or services and who would also sign up other distributors. In this system, the up-line of distributors would receive commissions on the distributors below them.

Power Team The people you have a relationship with, are in your Contact Sphere, and you are actively engaging with in a referral relationship.

Referral A recommendation of a person or business to someone who has a need for your products or services and is willing to connect.

Referral Marketing Referral Marketing is a business strategy to attract new customers or clients through a process of building relationships, which results in a flow of personally recommended business.

Referral Partners Referral Partners are members of your Power Team that meet ALL six criteria of a Referral Source:

1. Want, or can be inspired, to help you;
2. Have time, or are willing to make the time, to help you;
3. Have the ability, or can be trained, to do the things you want them to do;
4. Have the resources necessary to help you;
5. Have relationships with the types of people you want to target; and
6. Will make good referrals for people you know.

Viral Marketing This term refers to marketing techniques that use pre-existing social networks to produce increases in brand awareness or to achieve other marketing objectives (such as product sales) through self-replicating viral processes. This is the trend where everyone is talking about the latest fashion, movie, or hot spot. This is also sometimes used in conjunction with Buzz Marketing.

Word-of-Mouth Marketing Sometimes used in conjunction with Buzz Marketing, this is simply what people are saying about your products or services. A word-of-mouth marketing plan would have an effective message, delivered through identified Referral Sources to a targeted audience.

About the Authors

Dr. Ivan Misner is the Founder and Chairman of BNI, the world's largest business networking organization. BNI was founded in 1985. The organization now has thousands of chapters throughout every populated continent of the world. Each year, BNI generates millions of referrals, resulting in billions of dollars worth of business for its members.

Dr. Misner's Ph.D. is from the University of Southern California. He has written over a dozen books, including his *New York Times* bestseller, *Masters of Networking,* as well as his recent #1 bestseller, *The 29% Solution.* He is a monthly columnist for Entrepreneur.com and is the Senior Partner for the Referral Institute, a referral training company with trainers around the world. In addition, he has taught business management and social capital courses at several universities throughout the United States.

Called the "Father of Modern Networking" by CNN and the "Networking Guru" by *Entrepreneur* magazine, Dr. Misner is considered to be one of the world's leading experts on business networking and has been a keynote speaker for major corporations and associations throughout the world. He has been featured in the *L.A. Times, Wall Street Journal,* and *New York Times,* as well as numerous TV and radio shows on CNN, CNBC, and the BBC in London.

Dr. Misner is on the Board of Trustees for the University of LaVerne. He is also the Founder of the BNI-Misner Charitable Foundation and was recently named *"Humanitarian of the Year"* by a Southern California newspaper. He is married and lives with his wife Elisabeth and their three children in Claremont, California. ***In his spare time(!!!),*** he is also an amateur magician and a black belt in karate.

 **Mike Macedonio** is the President and Partner of the Referral Institute. He helps entrepreneurs and sales professionals build their businesses through qualified referrals. By implementing proven referral marketing strategies, clients working with Mike Macedonio and the Referral Institute are experiencing record sales growth, regardless of economic conditions.

Mike co-authored the book, *Truth or Delusion, Busting Networking's Biggest Myths*, with Ivan Misner, which has hit several bestseller lists, including *The New York Times, The Wall Street Journal, USA Today*, and Amazon.

Mike's position within the Referral Institute began as a trainer in 2001. In 2003, Mike was hand selected to be the President of the Referral Institute. Since that time, Mike has led the Referral Institute from a handful of trainers to a franchised organization operating throughout North America, Australia, Asia, and Europe.

Mike gives back to his community by volunteering. He holds a position on the Board of Directors for LIFT, a non-profit project to combat teen obesity, and is on the Board of Directors for the Wisconsin Big Cat Rescue, a non-profit caring for abused or neglected big cats.

When he is not helping entrepreneurs, teens, and big cats, Mike has an incredible passion for his wife, mountain climbing, and cycling.

REFERRAL®
INSTITUTE

The Referral Institute provides the training and tools to help business professionals gain financial success through relationship-based referral marketing. Our "Referrals for Life'" program is not a numbers game — it is not about spending hours making cold calls, collecting business cards, or developing a huge database of prospective customers. We don't want you to work harder to gain new business — we want you to learn how to work smarter. With the Referrals for Life® program, business referrals do not happen by accident. They result from implementing, and then consistently monitoring, a well-organized referral marketing plan.

The Referral Institute is an international franchised referral training and consulting company with locations in Australia, the Middle East, Europe, and North America. At The Referral Institute, we'll teach you how to make all your business relationships become more valuable to you and your business. As a result, you'll not only enjoy an increased quality of life because your business is flourishing, but you will also gain lifelong relationships: Referrals for Life®.

If you are a motivated business professional serious about moving your business to the next level, don't wait to contact the Referral Institute headquarters nearest to you.

Please go to www.referralinstitute.com to learn more about referral marketing, as well as how to attend a Referral Institute training program in your area. You may contact the organization at info@referralinstitute. com to talk about growing your business by generating qualified referrals.

BNI, the world's largest business networking organization, was founded by Dr. Ivan Misner in 1985 as a way for businesspeople to generate referrals in a structured, professional environment. The organization, now the world's largest referral business network, has thousands of chapters with tens of thousands of members on every populated continent. Since its inception, BNI members have passed millions of referrals, generating billions of dollars in business for the participants.

The primary purpose of the organization is to pass qualified business referrals to its members. The philosophy of BNI may be summed up in two simple words: Givers Gain˙. If you give business to people, you will get business from them. BNI allows only one person per profession to join a chapter. The program is designed to help businesspeople develop long-term relationships, thereby creating a basis for trust and, inevitably, referrals. The mission of BNI is to help members increase their business through a structured, positive, and professional word-of-mouth program that enables them to develop long-term, meaningful relationships with quality business professionals.

To visit a chapter near you, contact BNI via email at bni@bni.com or visit its website at www.bni.com.

Index